THE CRY OF THE DEER

David Adam is the Vicar of Holy Island. He has a particular interest in Celtic Christian traditions, of which he detects traces still lingering on in the Northern Church, and he is a composer of modern prayers in the Celtic tradition, a selection of which has been published under the title of *The Edge of Glory*. Much of the material in this present book originated in retreats which the author has conducted in churches and with other small groups. He has also since written *Tides and Seasons: Modern prayers in the Celtic tradition* and *The Eye of the Eagle: Meditations on the Hymn 'Be thou my vision'*.

THE CRY OF THE DEER

DAVID ADAM

*Illustrated by Peter Dingle
and Jenny Pearson*

TRI∆NGLE

First published 1987
Triangle/SPCK
Holy Trinity Church
Marylebone Road
London NW1 4DU

Fourth impression 1991

British Library Cataloguing in Publication Data

Adam, David, 1936–
    The cry of the deer: meditations on
    the hymn of St. Patrick.
1. Devotional literature
I. Title
    242   BV4832.2

    ISBN 0–281–04284–5

Printed in Great Britain by
BPCC Hazell Books
Aylesbury, Bucks, England
Member of BPCC Ltd.

*To Arline
and her attitude*

*To Kathryn
and her Carmina*

Contents

ACKNOWLEDGEMENTS

I would like to thank Peter Dingle for the majority of drawings in this book. Thanks also to Jenny Pearson for the rest of the drawings. May they both continue to enjoy the mysteries that life weaves around all of us.

My thanks to Will Taylor who has provided the cover. Between his home and mine are three fields and the mystical Presence that he so often portrays.

Without the dedication of Sharon Artley this book might never have been written. I am especially grateful to her and her word-processor.

As ever I need to record my indebtedness to Denise who keeps my theological musings well and truly earthed.

INTRODUCTION

The life of St Patrick, and his ability to rise over insurmountable odds, bear witness to the power of the God in whom he put his trust.

Patrick was born about AD 414[1] near the western coastline of the Roman province of Britannia, most likely near the shortest sea route from Ireland, and opposite Ulster. This would place his home somewhere between the Antonine Wall and Hadrian's Wall. It has often been claimed that the Dumbarton area around the Clyde is the best contender. The only place name that Patrick mentions is *Bannaven Taburniae*. This is now usually read as *Banna Venta Burniae*, and suggests a local market or centre (*venta*) near the Roman fort of *Banna*, what is now Birdoswald on the line of Hadrian's Wall. *Berniae* is 'of Bernia', which is the name of the district added for precision; *bern* was British for a mountain pass, and would be used later to give the name to the whole area of Bernicia.

When Patrick was only sixteen, he was captured by a raiding party from Ireland and sold as a slave to a petty king in Armagh. In an instant, the privileges of home, securities of position, plans for the future were gone. But somehow he was able to meet up with fellow Christians, possibly slaves like himself. It would have been easy to despair, to curse God and ask to die: but this is the time when Patrick's faith, and his personal relationship with God, were greatly strengthened. In his *Confessions* he writes:

> After I came to Ireland—and so tended sheep every day, I often prayed in the daytime . . . up to a hundred prayers and at night nearly as many, and I stayed in the forest, and on the mountains and before daylight I used to be roused to prayer in snow, and in frost and rain, and I felt no harm, nor was there any inclination to take things easily in me, because as I see now the Spirit seethed in me.[2]

Through constant prayer he built his living relationship with God. He knew he was not alone; and he triumphed, not in his own might, but in the power and presence of God. 'The Spirit seethed in me' is a lovely way of expressing his enthusiasm, his love for life.

Enthusiasm is something often lacking in our society today. In his play *Look Back in Anger*, John Osborne makes Jimmy Porter say:

> How I long for just a little ordinary, human enthusiasm. Just enthusiasm, that's all. I want to hear a warm thrilling voice cry out 'Hallelujah! Hallelujah! I'm alive!' . . . Oh brother it's such a long time since I was with anyone who got so enthusiastic about anything.[3]

Enthusiasm comes from two Greek words meaning 'in God'. There is no doubt that Patrick's life was in God and God in him. It is this awareness of God we will seek also in this book, so that we too may 'arise today' in His presence. Through the exercises at the end of each chapter, we will seek to discover that we dwell in Him and He in us.

No doubt, Patrick's faith let him never lose hope. Often he dreamed of escape. After six years the opportunity came and it is believed that he returned home. But Ireland had already captured him in other ways; he had dreams in which he seemed to hear his friends and the Irish calling to him: 'We pray thee, boy, to come and henceforth walk among us.' In spite of pleas from his kinsfolk, and the dangers of being put to death as a runaway slave, Patrick was determined to return as a missionary to Ireland.

He must have reached Ireland again in about 455. In his *Confessions* he gives as his reason for returning that he needed to expiate the sins of his youth by preaching the Gospel in Ireland. Columba's reason for leaving Ireland is said to have been the same. There is no doubt that the driving force behind Patrick's return was the Living God. Patrick speaks of his faith as an inner experience:

And another time I saw Him praying inside me as it

seemed . . . so I believe!—because of His indwelling Spirit, which has worked in me ever since that day.[4]

For a while Patrick seems to have worked as a layman, although it is possible that he had already been ordained by that time. He relates how he met Christians on his travels in Ireland even in remote regions 'where no-one had yet come to baptise'. Later, it seemed, he went to Gaul for training and ordination. This time when he returned he came to Tara, 'the centre of witchcraft and idolatry in Ireland'. Here was a test for Patrick and the future of Christianity in Ireland; here the new religion would confront the old ways.

When Easter approached, Patrick was determined to keep the festival in Tara: the feast of the Risen Lord was a time to rise over the heathen. As it happened, it coincided with a great pagan festival at Tara: all lights were to be extinguished and all fires put out, only the king would provide people with light and fire. Patrick and his companions pitched their tent, collected wood and kindled the Paschal fire, which lit up the whole of Mag Breg, so that the king's wise men warned him that unless the fire was extinguished immediately it would flood Ireland with its light and burn until Doomsday. They warned, speaking of Patrick: 'He goes around the Munster men and preaches to them and baptises them and leaves them clerics and churches . . .', and 'This is the shaven head and the falsifier who is deceiving every-one. Let us go and attack him and see if his God will help him.'

The king was in no doubt that Patrick had to be stopped: 'We will go and slay the man who has kindled this fire.' Soldiers were sent to capture Patrick and prevent him from coming to Tara; they surrounded him and his men. When Patrick saw them, he quoted the Psalms: 'Some put their trust in chariots and some in horses; but we in the Lord our God.' He was able to escape his attackers, came to no harm and entered Tara itself.

In the eyes of the people there was no doubt that the power of this new religion was greater than theirs. Legend grew that Patrick was more powerful than the Druids, that he was a 'shape-changer'. It was said that when the army attacked him, Patrick turned himself into a deer and so escaped them. Whatever we make of that, tradition says that this is when he composed the hymn known as 'The Deer's Cry' or 'The Breastplate of St Patrick'.

The prayer as we know it may belong to three centuries after Patrick, but that does not matter. It expresses so well much of the early Celtic Christian Faith. It vibrates still with the God who surrounds us, the Christ who is with us, and the Spirit within us. In these affirmations, the Divine Glory is woven into all of life like a fine thread; there is a Presence and a Power that pervades everything. Today, that same Presence continues to vibrate with glory for all who have eyes to see and ears to hear. The glory is not something we create, it is God's gift of Himself to us. It is a mystery to be enjoyed, not a problem to be solved. Let us set out to enjoy Him, His Presence and Power.

There are two translations of the affirmation that I like— Kuno Meyer's, entitled 'The Deer's Cry', and Mrs C. F. Alexander's hymn 'St Patrick's Breastplate' set to the tune 'St Patrick'. I have included both for your reading after this Introduction.

After entering Tara, Patrick set out to preach: 'I will go that I may show my readiness before the men of Ireland. It is not a "candle under a vat" that I will make of myself.' Soon he was to be found wandering all over Ireland, preaching, baptising and building churches. His courage and faith did not fail him. He has been described as a lion in boldness, a serpent in cunning and a laborious servant of the Creator.

When asked by the two daughters of Leoghain, King of Connaught, 'Who is your God and where is He?' Patrick, filled with Holy Spirit replied:

> Our God is the God of all, God of Heaven and earth, sea and river. He has His dwelling in heaven and earth and sea and all that are therein. He inspires all things; He quickens all things. He kindles the light of the sun and of the moon. He has a Son, co-eternal with Himself and like unto Him. And the Holy Spirit breathes in them. Father, Son and Holy Spirit are not divided. I desire to unite you to the Son of the Heavenly King, for you are daughters of a king of earth.[5]

May the same God inspire us as inspired Patrick: may we bind our lives to His, that we may 'arise today'.

THE HYMN OF
ST PATRICK

The Deer's Cry

Kuno Meyer's translation[1]

I arise today
Through a mighty strength, the invocation of the
  Trinity,
Through belief in the threeness,
Through confession of the oneness
Of the Creator of Creation.

I arise today
Through the strength of Christ's birth with his baptism,
Through the strength of his crucifixion with his burial,
Through the strength of his resurrection with his
  ascension,
Through the strength of his descent for the judgement
  of Doom.

I arise today
Through the strength of the love of the Cherubim,
In the obedience of angels,
In the service of archangels,
In the hope of the resurrection to meet with reward,
In the prayers of patriarchs,
In prediction of prophets,
In preaching of apostles,
In faith of confessors,
In innocence of holy virgins,
In deeds of righteous men.

I arise today
Through the strength of heaven;
Light of sun,
Radiance of moon,
Splendour of fire,

Speed of lightning,
Swiftness of wind,
Depth of sea,
Stability of earth,
Firmness of rock.

I arise today
Through God's strength to pilot me:
God's might to uphold me,
God's wisdom to guide me,
God's eye to look before me,
God's ear to hear me,
God's word to speak to me,
God's hand to guard me,
God's way to lie before me,
God's shield to protect me,
God's host to save me,
From snares of devils,
From temptations of vices,
From every one who shall wish me ill,
Afar and anear,
Alone and in a multitude.

I summon today all these powers between me and those
  evils,
Against every cruel merciless power that may oppose my
  body and soul,
Against incantations of false prophets,
Against black laws of pagandom,
Against false laws of heretics,
Against craft of idolatry,
Against spells of women and smiths and wizards,
Against every knowledge that corrupts man's body and
  soul.

Christ to shield me today
Against poisoning, against burning,
Against drowning, against wounding,
So there come to me abundance of reward.
Christ with me, Christ before me, Christ behind me,
Christ in me, Christ beneath me, Christ above me,
Christ on my right, Christ on my left,
Christ when I lie down, Christ when I sit down, Christ
    when I arise,
Christ in the heart of every man who thinks of me,
Christ in the mouth of every one who speaks of me,
Christ in the eye of every one that sees me,
Christ in every ear that hears me.

I arise today
Through a mighty strength, the invocation of the
    Trinity,
Through belief in the threeness,
Through confession of the oneness
Of the Creator of Creation.

St Patrick's Breastplate

[C. F. Alexander's translation[2]]

I bind unto myself today
The strong name of the Trinity,
By invocation of the same,
The Three in One and One in Three.

I bind this day to me for ever,
By power of faith, Christ's Incarnation;
His baptism in the Jordan River;
His death on cross for my salvation;
His bursting from the spicèd tomb;
His riding up the heavenly way;
His coming at the day of doom;
I bind unto myself today.

I bind unto myself the power
Of the great love of the Cherubim;
The sweet 'Well done' in judgement hour;
The service of the Seraphim,
Confessors' faith, Apostles' word,
The Patriarchs' prayers, the Prophets' scrolls.
All good deeds done unto the Lord,
And purity of virgin souls.

I bind unto myself today
The virtues of the starlit heaven,
The glorious sun's life-giving ray,
The whiteness of the moon at even,
The flashing of the lightning free,
The whirling wind's tempestuous shocks,
The stable earth, the deep salt sea,
Around the old eternal rocks.

I bind unto myself today
The power of God to hold and lead,
His eye to watch, His might to stay,
His ear to hearken to my need.
The wisdom of my God to teach,
His hand to guide, his shield to ward;
The word of God to give me speech,
His heavenly host to be my guard.

Against the demon snares of sin,
The vice that gives temptation force,
The natural lusts that war within,
The hostile men that mar my course;
Or few or many, far or nigh,
In every place, and in all hours
Against their fierce hostility,
I bind to me these holy powers.

Against all Satan's spells and wiles,
Against false words of heresy,
Against the knowledge that defiles
Against the heart's idolatry,
Against the wizard's evil craft,
Against the death-wound and the burning
The choking wave and poisoned shaft,
Protect me, Christ, till thy returning.

Christ be with me, Christ within me,
Christ behind me, Christ before me,
Christ beside me, Christ to win me,
Christ to comfort and restore me,
Christ beneath me, Christ above me,
Christ in quiet, Christ in danger,
Christ in hearts of all that love me,
Christ in mouth of friend and stranger.

I bind unto myself the name,
The strong name of the Trinity;
By invocation of the same.
The Three in One, and One in Three,
Of whom all nature hath creation;
Eternal Father, Spirit, Word:
Praise to the Lord of my salvation,
Salvation is of Christ the Lord.

STRENGTH THROUGH FAITH

P. Dingle

Strength through Faith

I arise today
Through a mighty strength, the invocation of the Trinity.

Life had been getting increasingly hard, so I ran away.
For a while at least, I would escape; I went into the
Cheviot Hills. The morning was spent winding down,
watching the dipper on the River Breamish and a buzzard
circling on the air currents. The afternoon was filled with
the sound of the cuckoo. Suddenly the valley darkened;
it was only a cloud, but all my troubles returned with it.
The beauties of the valley were still there, but I could no
longer see them or hear them; I was distracted, out of
tune. Perhaps if I climbed the hill tops I would see the
sun again.

In a while I reached the summit, climbing over a great
heap of stones into a Bronze Age fortress. I sat in this
great circle of stones to get my breath back, and looked
out towards the North Sea in the direction of Holy Island.
A great storm was brewing and coming my way. I watched
the louring clouds racing towards the hills, yet they never
came. The hills seemed to break the clouds and divide
them: the storm went to the north and south, but it did
not come over me. In that ancient circle built to protect
ancient man, I suddenly felt protected. I was surrounded
by the Presence and Power of God. He would not leave
me or forsake; I could not slip out of His love or care. The
words of a hymn came to mind, and I spoke them as an
act of faith:

> The storm may roar without me,
> My heart may low be laid,

> But God is round about me
> And can I be dismayed?

The Presence of God is an eternal fact. He never leaves us alone or forsakes us. It is when we lose sight of Him that we falter and sink beneath the waves. We need to regain a clear vision of the Presence, to perceive the reality of His relationship with us and act upon it.

Not long ago, I was in a little grey chapel in a valley. The preacher was rather tedious and the hymns dull. I could have endured both, but when he started his prayers by saying, 'Now I just want you to imagine God is present,' I could have wept. I now knew why it was such heavy going: he did not know of the Presence, he could only imagine it. God is beyond our greatest imagination; either He is present, and that influences everything we do, or He is absent, and then we are poor indeed.

Faith is the discovery that He is at hand: 'in Him we live and move and have our being.' Faith is the joy of knowing that we dwell in Him and He in us. You cannot imagine this, you cannot even make it happen, but you can experience it as a fact. It is necessary to keep ourselves sensitive, what the Celt calls 'to tune the five-stringed harp', to keep each of our five senses alert to the fact of God and His surrounding Presence. There, in the Cheviot Hills, I became in tune once more. For a while I had lost sight of the beauty of the earth; no wonder I was blind to the glories of the Presence. Now all came back to me as I opened myself to them. I made an affirmation of my faith to the God who is about me and said aloud:

> Circle me O God
> Keep hope within
> Despair without.

Circle me O God
Keep peace within
Keep turmoil out.

Circle me O God
Keep calm within
Keep storms without.

Circle me O God
Keep strength within
Keep weakness out.[1]

Here I rediscovered a power and a strength that was not my own: I turned to God who knows that we have no power of ourselves. I had discovered what the Celtic people call the *Caim*, the Encircling.

It is said that when the Celtic saints were troubled by evil or attacked by enemies, they drew the *Caim* around them. Sometimes they actually made a circle around themseves by using a stick or their index finger. This was no magic, but an expression of the reality of the Presence of God. The encompassing of any of the Three Persons of the Trinity, or all of them, might be called on. In old times the suppliant would stretch out the right hand with the index finger extended, while turning around sunwise, as if on a pivot, and calling for the desired Presence to protect him. The circle was said to accompany the person on his journey and keep him from dangers.

This was a way of acting out the truth stated by Paul in Romans:

If God is for us, who can be against us? . . .
I am certain that nothing can separate us from his love:
    neither death nor life,
neither angels nor other heavenly rulers or powers,
neither the present nor the future,
neither the world above or the world below—there is

13

nothing in all creation that will ever be able to separate us from the love of God
which is ours through Christ Jesus our Lord.[2]

Once this becomes our own personal experience, life becomes quite different. The *Caim* works, not as a charm, but to re-tune us to the reality of the love and presence of God. I like to listen to my transistor in the morning to hear the news. When I first come into the room all is silent, the radio waves are there, but I have not switched on; the transistor does not create the music, it only receives it. I need to switch on and be tuned in. So it is with the Divine Presence. By calling upon Him, we tune ourselves to His being with us.

The Hymn of St Patrick is used like a *Caim*:

> *I arise today*
> *Through a mighty strength, the invocation*
> *Of the Trinity.*

Call upon the Father; take your time. You may like to see yourself as if a child with a heavy load to carry. You have been struggling with this, feeling that it will defeat you; it is too heavy for you, it is wearing you out. The Father is there. Call upon Him. He has been watching and waiting. He will not only help you to carry your load; He will carry you if you are weary. Call upon Him. Let His arms enfold you, His love surround you.

> The encircling God is with you,
> The encircling Power of the Creator.

Call upon the Saviour. It is when we are unable to help ourselves that we begin to know Christ as our Saviour. Call upon Him who has conquered death and all the hells of this world. With His wounded hands He will enfold you. He calls you: 'Come to me all of you who are tired

from carrying heavy loads, and I will give you rest.'³
Come, trust in Him.

> The enfolding of Christ be round you,
> The enfolding arms of His love.

Come to the Lord and giver of Life. Come to the Spirit,
who transforms you from a 'lump of clay' to a living being,
a person. Come to the Spirit to be refreshed, renewed,
restored.

> The encompassing of the Spirit be round you,
> The encompassing of the strength of God.

This is how to begin the day, not in your own effort,
but in the power of God. Awake to this fact and it will
help you to arise—not only to get up, but to get over
so many things that would pull you down. The way to
overcome gravity—and so much triviality—is to arise in
the Presence each morning. To know that we are the sons
and daughters of God, that He is with us and that He gives
us life eternal. He gives today a resurrection quality, and
helps us to *arise*. St Paul says of this:

> We who have this spiritual treasure are like common
> clay pots, in order to show that the supreme power
> belongs to God, not us. We are often troubled, but
> not crushed; sometimes in doubt, but never in despair;
> there are many enemies, but we are never without a
> friend; and though badly hurt at times, we are not
> destroyed.⁴

Because such prayers are like pulling a coat around us
when the weather becomes severe, many of them became
dressing prayers. They were like St Paul putting on 'the
whole armour of God'. In her translation of the St
Patrick's Breastplate, Mrs Alexander makes it sound as if
Patrick is fastening the Presence to himself: binding God

to him as carefully as he binds on his shoes or his tunic. Perhaps as he was dressing he would say:

> *I bind unto myself today*
> *The strong name of the Trinity,*
> *By invocation of the same,*
> *The Three in One and One in Three.*

As he threads the laces through the eye-holes of his tunic and pulls them tight about his body, he continues:

> *I bind this day to me for ever,*
> *By power of faith, Christ's Incarnation;*
> *His baptism in the Jordan River;*
> *His death on cross for my salvation.*

This is not a God of the remote past, a historical God, nor is it a God of the distant future, but a God who is near at hand ready to help. He is our God *today*. It is today that we are able to meet Him.

Sometimes such prayer has been compared with the modern idea of positive thinking, but is is far more than that. Positive thinking is dangerously near to suggesting that we are self-sufficient, that it is all in the mind and we are always able to help ourselves. Life in the end must always prove this to be a lie. The *Caim* and dressing prayers are putting our trust in a power beyond ourselves. Positive thinking tends to be egocentric; our prayers are God-centred, discovering that we are centred in God, without whom nothing is strong.

David Gascoyne expresses it so well:

> Always, whenever, whatever, however,
> When I am able to resist
> For once the constant pressure of failure to exist

Let me remember
That to be truly man is to be man aware of thee
And unafraid to be. So help me God.[5]

EXERCISES

1. *Pause in the Presence.* 'In the beginning God.' This is how the Bible begins, and this is how prayer must begin. Words without the Presence remain just words, but we are not without the Presence. Let the Word become flesh and dwell among us that we may behold His glory.

In the Beginning GOD

> In the beginning of space
> of time
> of the universe, GOD.
>
> In the beginning of creation
> of life
> of mankind, GOD.
>
> In the beginning of individuals
> of personalities
> of me, GOD.
>
> In the beginning of this year
> of this week
> of this hour, GOD.
>
> In the beginning of each thought
> of each word
> of each deed, GOD.

Add to this any beginnings you feel are important to you this day. Know that He abides with you and surrounds you.

'As He was in the beginning, He is now and shall be forever, God.' Amen.

2. *Practise the Caim.* Know that we dwell in Him and He in us.

> Your Presence is in my life
> Your Presence is all around me
> Your Presence is Peace.

Your Presence is in my house
Your Presence is all around me
Your Presence is Peace.

Your Presence is in my work
Your Presence is all around me
Your Presence is Peace.[6]

Choose new statements in the first line to express where you need to affirm His Presence. Make them really personal; your Presence is in the tube (underground), on the bus, in the factory . . .

Change the last word of the last line. Substitute whatever gift of the Presence you seek—'your Presence is love . . . joy . . . strength . . . healing . . . restoring.' But do use the same phrase often: not to make it happen, but to know it is already true.

You may like to make a circle when you begin, knowing that God does encircle you. Like a ripple caused by a stone on a pond, you may like to ever increase your circle. Start with yourself, your home, your street, and move ever outward. Picture each in turn surrounded also by the Love, Peace and Presence of God.

3. *The 5p exercise* This is a good exercise for beginners. I have called it the '5p Exercise', because each part can be described by a word beginning with 'P'.

Pause, Presence, Picture, Ponder, Promise

Pause   Stop what you are doing. Let yourself relax; let all the tension go out of your body, all troubled thoughts out of your mind . . . Make space in your life for something to happen . . . Make room for God.
Let go, and let God.
Breathe slowly and deeply . . .
Be still . . .

Presence   . . . know that God is with you.

This is the purpose of this exercise—to discover that God is with you.

'God unseen yet ever near
Thy Presence may I feel.'

The Presence is to be enjoyed.

Let God take over . . . Do not try to do anything at this stage but to be aware of Him and rest in His Presence. Make little acts of affirmation.

'Lord you are here. Help me to know it'

'Lord you are love. Help me to receive you.'

Picture   what this fact of Presence means for you today. Your God is with you: you dwell in Him and He in you. He is with you at work, at rest, at play.

Ponder   Think what this should mean for each of those situations.

We are never alone. There is an abiding Presence; strength, love, peace, forgiveness are ever at hand.

'My Presence will go with you and I will give you rest.'

Promise   to recall the fact of His Presence throughout the day, perhaps by using the *Caim*. Promise:

*'I will arise today,
Through a mighty strength, the invocation of the Trinity'.*

TO SEE CHRIST

To See Christ

I arise today
Through the strength of Christ's birth with his baptism.

The Incarnation is a glorious mystery to be enjoyed! In every age it has expressed the love of God for the world, His coming to us and being involved with us. It is the greatest expression of a God who is not far off. Our God is not proud; He comes down and is among us.

That God could take upon Him our flesh and dwell among us will remain for ever beyond our comprehension. As a problem, the Incarnation will never come to a definite conclusion. But that is to do with the limits of our minds and not the limits of God. If we would restrict God to our way of thinking, He must be a very small god indeed.

Many people find it easier to begin with the love of God for us, rather than the birth at Bethlehem. Begin by knowing that God cares for His world and is deeply involved in it. In comprehension He transcends our little minds, but in love He is immanent. God is at hand, waiting to be discovered.

> Lift the stone and you will find me
> Cleave the wood and I am there.

Once you believe and begin to experience the Presence, the Incarnation is then to be seen as yet another way of God's communicating with us. 'The Word was made flesh and dwelt among us, and we beheld His glory.'[1] The coming of God in Christ Jesus is a unique event in all its fullness and it is still the way to the heart of God—through Jesus Christ our Lord.

For many today the way to God is through service, through caring, through loving our brothers and sisters. This can be a way to discover the Incarnation, the Divine in our midst. This is expressed simply, but very well in the little verse:

> I sought my God
> My God I could not see.
> I sought my soul
> My soul eluded me.
> I sought my brother
> And I found all three.

St Martin of Tours influenced the Celtic Church by the form of mission and monastic settlement he helped to establish in Gaul. Here, one of the founding fathers of the Celtic Church, St Ninian, received some of his training. There is no doubt that the vision of St Martin was something the early Church treasured: a vision of 'Christ in friend and stranger'.

Whilst still in the Roman army and preparing to become a Christian, Martin was stationed near Amiens. One cold day, he went out with his soldier companions. They wore heavy cloaks to protect them from the bitter weather. Their cloaks were among their prized possessions. As they approached the city gates, they met a beggar who was near naked and about to perish with the cold. As soon as he saw him, Martin was moved with compassion. He drew his sword and cut his cloak in two, giving one part to the beggar. His companions jeered and mocked him for his foolishness; they would not let him forget such folly in a hurry. That night Martin had a vision. He saw into the kingdom of heaven, and there was Christ surrounded by angels. Christ was wearing the cloak that Martin had given to the beggar. Martin heard Christ say, 'Look, this is the cloak which Martin has given to me this day'. Martin had discovered the great secret of God Incarnate. The Incarnation, though unique in Christ Jesus, is not a past event, but an eternal event. The Incarnation is continuous and is there for us to experience.

Other experiences that are well known are those of St Christopher and St Francis. Christopher struggled across the ford with a child on his shoulders. The child needed help, and Christopher gave it. On reaching the other bank, Christopher put the child down and proceeded to dry himself. During this time the child disappeared—likely went off home. Perhaps in later years Christopher could have put a name to that child, but that night he knew it was Christ! It was from that incident that he took the delightful name of Christ-bearer—Christopher.

St Francis sought to express the love of God in all of creation. This was not too difficult with the birds and the flowers. It was hard when he was confronted with a leper covered in sores. Suddenly, Francis was faced with an outcast from society, scorned and rejected of men. With a great effort, he took the leper in his arms, and then knew that he embraced Christ and Christ embraced him. Each of these saints discovered the sacrament of the Divine Presence in a fellow being: 'whenever you did this for one of the least important of these brothers of mine, you did it for me!'[2]

The Celtic Church celebrates St Bride's Day in February. There are many legends about her and the Christ child, and I believe they are told to keep us aware of the mystical Presence that comes to us. Here is one of them.

A great famine had come upon the land. The parents of Bride were forced to leave home and go to look for food. The little lass was left to look after the house, with only a 'single stoup of water and a bannock of bread.' There were the usual warnings from parents: to be careful with the

25

food for that was all there was, and not to let any strangers into the house. Late that very night, as the light faded into the gloaming, two travellers came down the lane. One was an old man, the other a maid. It was said that the old man had brown hair and a grey beard; the woman was young and very beautiful. They asked for food and a place to rest. Bride felt sorry for them, but she knew she must obey her parents, and not invite them in. She shared with them her water and her bread, then took them round the back of the house to the barn and helped them make it comfortable. When she returned to the front of the house, there she found the bannock was whole again and the water stoup full. She knew in her heart that she had been dealing with more than mere man. When she looked out again, night had fallen, but the stable was surrounded by a brilliant golden light for *Christ had come to earth*.

Jesus said, 'I was a stranger and you received me in your homes'. The legend of St Bride is about a way of seeing; a way of experiencing 'the Word made flesh'; that we may see Christ in others. There is a Celtic Rune of Hospitality used by the Iona Community and by Kenneth MacLeod which says:

> I saw a stranger at yestere'en.
> I put food in the eating place,
> drink in the drinking place,
> music in the listening place,
> and in the sacred name of
>   the Triune
> He blessed myself and my house,
> my cattle and my dear ones,
> and the lark said in her song
> often, often, often,
> goes the Christ in the stranger's guise.

To be able to make room in your life for another—especially a stranger—is a great gift. We need to teach ourselves to give others our undivided attention. Often we call, 'There is no room at the inn'; no room in our hearts, minds or homes. It is when we open ourselves to the other who comes to us that the great Other also seeks to enter our lives. Jesus still says, 'Where two or three come together . . . I am there.'

To see Christ in others is the beginning of a great adventure: to discover that we do not possess Him, but that He comes and possesses us. We do not have to bring Christ to people to discover His Presence in them. In typical Orthodox fashion, Turgenev describes this experience in one of his prose poems. It is what he experienced in a low-pitched wooden church as a boy. He is surrounded by icons of saints and glowing candles.

All at once some man came up and stood beside me.
I did not turn towards him: but at once felt that this
    man was Christ.
Emotion, curiosity, awe overmastered me suddenly.
I made an effort . . . and looked at my neighbour.
A face like everyone's, a face like all men's faces . . .
What sort of Christ is this? I thought.
I turned away. But I had hardly turned my eyes from
    this ordinary man when I felt again that it was really
    none other than Christ standing beside me.
Again I made an effort over myself . . .
And again the same face, like all men's faces, the same
    everyday, though unknown, features.
And suddenly my heart sank, and I came to myself.
Only then I realised that just such a face—a face like all
    men's faces—is the face of Christ.[3]

There was one Good Friday when I had a Three Hours' service to take in Middlesbrough. I left home rather late.

As I came out of the village of Castleton there was a large hill to climb. As I drove up it, I saw a local man struggling with a railway sleeper; where he was going, I do not know. I sped on my way. The nearer I got to Middlesbrough, the more I was bothered. I had seen a man struggling up a hill with a weight of wood. It was Good Friday. I had seen the Christ and passed Him by! I know that man by name, I meet him still; but I know that in him I also met Christ. 'Whenever you did this for the least important of these . . . you did it for me!'

The Incarnation is about a God who comes, who 'invades' our world and is to be discovered among us. It is not that we possess Him, it is that He possesses us.

Too often the Church talks as if it possessed God, as if it could produce Him at will. With some people, there is a danger of feeling that we can produce Him like a white rabbit from the folds of our coat or from the leaves of a book; that He is something we own and can give to others. It is at such a point that Christ seems to do the vanishing trick! The Church has got caught in an imperialist role, saying to others, 'I have this, and I know what is good for you. Without what I have, you are poor and ignorant— not to forget damned! I have the riches to bring to your poverty, I am the possessor of what you need to receive.' Unfortunately, this has been the approach that destroyed rich cultures and beautiful treasures of other lands. Because we failed to listen to and to see the other, we failed to receive their riches; a wealth of spirituality has been lost to us.

With the Celtic Church it was different. The Celtic Church did not so much seek to bring Christ as to discover Him: not to possess Him, but to see Him in 'friend and stranger'; to liberate the Christ who is already there in all His riches. This is a very different way from the imperialist: it is to sit humbly and accept the other who comes to

28

you, to share with him and learn from him. It is not the way of the conqueror, but of the explorer and discoverer.

The ancient poems 'The Lyke Wake Dirge' is about how we respond to others, and that is how we will be judged. The poem is obviously based on Matthew 25. 31-46. Here are four verses:

If ever thou gavest hosen and shoon
—Every night and all,
Sit thee down and put them on;
And Christ receive thy soul.

If hosen and shoon thou ne'er gavest nane
—Every night and all,
The whins shall prick thee to the bare bane;
And Christ receive thy soul.

If ever thou gavest meat and drink
—Every night and all,
The fire shall never make thee shrink;
And Christ receive thy soul.

If meat and drink thou ne'er gavest nane
—Every night and all,
The fire will burn thee to the bare bane;
And Christ receive thy soul.

The Incarnation involves us in social responsibility. It is a challenge to our way of life. It is in the cry of the poor that Christ still calls to us; in the call of the other that He comes to us.

From the Incarnation—God with us—it is an easy step to baptism, the total immersion into the Father, Son and Holy Spirit. When it comes to baptism, I believe in total immersion, where the person is submerged, surrounded, completely covered. (But parents need not worry when they bring their children to baptism: I am not going to start dipping them in the font, nor am I going to take them down to the river! I will continue the symbolic sprinkling—but it is a symbol of the total immersion.)

Too many people are just sprinkled with Christianity—some would say immunised against the real thing; they have a little bit of faith, a few beliefs, some grasp of the story of Jesus. But it can hardly be called immersion. There are some who dip in now and again, when they feel like it—a strange sort of relationship with their God. It could hardly be called a 'love affair'.

No, I believe in total immersion—none of this half-hearted approach. Even on an everyday level, when the world is going mad and there is trouble all around, it is good to immerse yourself in something sensible like a book or a good play, or to get immersed in garden or sport—so that they involve your whole being. It is amazing how much energy we have to do the things we want to do!

Jesus said, *immerse* people everywhere in the name of the Father and of the Son and of the Holy Spirit. Everywhere, and at all times, immerse people in the Presence of the Creator, the Redeemer, the Strengthener. Like the Incarnation, Baptism is not a once-and-for-all event. It is a continuous process. You are not 'done', but forever renewing and re-doing. Like all relationships, to be immersed in the Trinity needs our constant attention and working at. Water baptism is only the beginning of the adventure of total immersion. We must daily, if not hourly, immerse ourselves, our children, our homes, our work, our world in the powers of the Sacred Three. This is not making the relationship happen, but becoming aware that it is a fact: 'we dwell in Him and He in us'.

EXERCISES

These exercises are about our awareness: what we give our attention to and what we are immersed in. Go over all your meetings with others today, and see if you let the Other enter your life.

1.   **We would see Christ**

> In the birth of a child
> In the love of a parent
> In the joining of lives
> > *We would see Christ.*

> In the meeting of a friend
> In the question of a stranger
> In the meeting with another
> > *We would see Christ.*

> In the journey on the train
> In the office's routine
> In the factory's production
> > *We would see Christ.*

Some people's minds are so closed to anything, that the Other has hardly a chance. If we are not open to those whom we see, how can we be open to Him who is unseen?

2.   **Be Opened**

> Lord open our lips;
> And our mouth shall declare your praise.

> Lord open our eyes;
> And we shall behold your glory in others.

> Lord open our hearts;
> And we shall discover your love in loving others.

> Lord open our lives;
> And all living shall declare your Presence.

Affirm regularly:

> You are the caller
> You are the poor
> You are the stranger at my door.
>
> You are the wanderer
> The unfed
> You are the homeless
> With no bed.
>
> You are the man
> Driven insane
> You are the child
> Crying in pain.
>
> You are the Other who comes to me.
> If I open to another, you're born in me.[4]

3. A prayer based on Teilhard de Chardin:

Give me to recognise in other men, Lord God, the radiance of your own face. The irresistible light of your eyes, shining in the depth of things . . . Grant me now to see you above all in the most inward, most perfect, most remote levels of the souls of my brothers.[5]

4. Continue to practise the *caim* by knowing you are immersed at all times in:

> the Peace of the Father
> the Love of the Son
> the Power of the Spirit

and let these gifts of the Presence spread out in prayer to others.

> *I arise today*
> *Through the strength of Christ's birth with his baptism.*

DEATH IS NOT FATAL

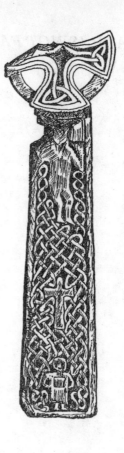

Death is Not Fatal

I arise today
Through the strength of his crucifixion with his burial.

Celtic and Anglo-Saxon stone crosses are full of symbolism and fascination. A favourite of mine is the cross at Stonegrave Minster near Helmsley in North Yorkshire. The shaft of the cross is covered with a typical interlacing in a criss-cross pattern: this represents life—it looks simple, but in fact is very complex. As the line travels over the whole of the shaft, it goes over and under, under and over itself, just as life has its ups and downs: sometimes you are on top of the world and at other times things get you down. If you follow this line, it is usually endless. For the Christian, that is a strong statement about life.

The criss-cross pattern also represents the weaving of life by the fates: the fact that our life is limited, our freedoms restricted. Like the stonemason, we are only able to work within fixed parameters. So much is already laid out, measured for us. Some would argue that we are in the hands of fate, predestined from the start. But the pattern is not allowed to take over. Fate does not have the last word. It is not the final explanation of life. Superimposed, bedded right into the pattern, are three figures. There is a majestically powerful figure at the top, holding up the pillars of the world. He is above all and has command. He looks like Atlas with the world, the wheeled cross-head, on his shoulders. He upholds us at all times.

At the base of the cross is a squared figure of a man holding a book. Often Celtic missionaries are shown with a book-satchel around their neck. Here is our guide and strengthener, the Spirit of God.

Central to the shaft is an empty cross, without the pattern of the fates. It is the sign of Jesus triumphant, neither the cross nor the grave could keep Him. He is let loose in the world. The message is that we are not in the hands of fate, but in the hands of the Almighty; death is not fatal.

In John 11. 4, where Jesus is trying to explain to the disciples about Lazarus, He says: 'The final result of this illness will not be the death of Lazarus . . . and it will be the means by which the Son of God will receive glory.' Jesus is trying to tell them that death is not the end, not a terminal disease; but it is hard to understand. In verse 11 of the same chapter, Jesus says: 'Our friend Lazarus has fallen asleep, but I will go and wake him up.' The disciples still find it difficult to comprehend, so Jesus says plainly, 'Lazarus is dead.' Still, He had promised to come and awaken him, and that He did. The Celtic Church was very much in the tradition of St John's Gospel—believing that death is a grave matter, but not fatal!

It is because Christians believe that death is not the end that they dare risk their lives and even court martyrdom. By their death, the martyrs witnessed fully to their faith in eternal life; death is but the gate to glory.

The Celtic Church had two different expressions of martyrdom—Red martyrdom and White martyrdom. Each bore witness in a different way to the power to survive death. Red martyrdom was the actual laying down of one's life for the faith. This was always possible in the early Church and in pagan society. These martyrs often faced death singing songs of praise and praying for their persecutors. They were strong witnesses for the resurrection, that death is not a terminus, but a step on the journey to the Promised Land. The blood of such martyrs was the seed of the Church.

But there are more deaths than physical death, and they can be every bit as traumatic. For the Celts, white martyrdom was having to go into exile for the gospel's sake. To leave clan and country was to risk death at all times. It was to become homeless, even nameless. Without the security and backing of the clan, you were a nobody. It meant leaving behind all the things you trusted in. Sometimes this martyrdom was put upon someone as a penance for an evil deed or an act of violence. St Columba was made to leave Ireland because he caused so many deaths. St Patrick said that he left home and returned to Ireland to expiate the sins of youth. Others became wanderers for God—to show 'that we are pilgrims and travellers on this earth, that here we have no abiding city': on this earth there are no gilt-edged securities.

This is not a gloomy outlook on life; far from it, it calls us to a life of adventure. It can be a shaking off of false securities. No longer possessed by possessions, we may become open enough to be possessed by God. Kirkegaard has said: 'It is good once in a while to feel oneself in the hands of God, and not always eternally slinking around the familiar nooks and corners of a town where one always knows the way out.'

In what I believe to be a rather humorous expression of this, we get in the *Anglo-Saxon Chronicle* for the year 891:

Three Scots came to King Alfred from Ireland in a boat without oars. They left their home bent on serving God in a state of pilgrimage, they did not care where. Their boat was made of two-and-a-half hides and contained enough provisions to last them seven days, and within a week came they and landed in Cornwall and shortly afterwards came to King Alfred. They were called Dubslane, Macbeth and Maelinmum.[1]

Whilst training at Kelham Theological College, I was privileged to capture a glimpse of this heroic way of living.

From the 'Principles' of the Society of the Sacred Mission, I learned:

> In regard to outer things, first it is necessary that you should exercise such self-mastery that there is nothing you cannot lay easily aside. You must leave all one day whether you will or not . . .
>
> If you have given your whole life to God, why should you prefer to lose it in this way rather than that? . . .
>
> If it cost you your life, what better could you ask than that the time of trial be very short, since the reward is the same?[2]

This attitude to life, far from impoverishing it, enriches it, frees it and makes it heroic. It is a way of looking at life more honestly and clearly and not getting caught with the false 'securities' of the world. We, in the twentieth century, need to recapture a vision of living daringly for our Lord, casting away our man-made securities and putting our trust in Him. We have been fooled into pretending we are self-sufficient and self-reliant. We are in danger of being 'the self-made man who worships his creator'. Perhaps we should remind ourselves where it all ends: *memento mori*, 'for death, there is no remedy in the garden'.

Now we are looking at a forbidden subject. Death is one of the taboos of our age. It is because we refuse to face it and its consequences that it has such a grip on many. We avoid not only the 'red' death, but the 'white' death, the 'change and decay' that is all around us. We work so hard at keeping things alive that should be allowed to die decently. We keep organisations alive that have passed their usefulness; we spend millions of pounds trying to sustain a past that is gone. We cover up with euphemisms and cosmetics. What we avoid at all costs is breakdown, which is looked upon as death. Breakdown is talked of in hushed tones, as if it were a deadly sin. There are countless people avoiding breakdown by tranquillising themselves one way or another. Breakdown often occurs when an old way of life or a relationship dies and we refuse to face it. We use our energies and resources to discover the 'good old days' and we are not at ease in the present. Being not at ease is often the precipitating factor of dis-ease, and disease can lead to death.

Look to the Cross. Jesus saw it coming, but He did not run away. He faced death, and the many deaths that flesh is heir to. He knew that a loved one would betray Him. He was betrayed with a kiss, deserted by His closest companions, disowned by His friend on whom He relied, left alone (yet not alone). He suffered mental, physical and spiritual agonies. He was crucified, dead and buried. His life could seem a complete breakdown, a total failure. But the Cross is empty. Breakdown is not the end. It is only part of the process of this earth. Without the cross there is no resurrection; without death, no newness of life. Without breakdown there is no breakthrough.

Too often I keep things that should be scrapped. I have an old petrol-driven lawn mover that costs me hours in repairs and money. I need to admit that it has broken down, instead of thinking it is breaking down. I need to admit it, so that I can renew it. So it is with life. We must say something is broken down; only then can it be repaired or renewed. So often it is not a breakdown we are having, but a breakthrough. If only we would see it, we are hesitating on the very edge of a new world for us. Stop saying, 'I'm having a breakdown'; say, 'I have already broken down and am experiencing a breakthrough'. Accept that our cross, breakdown, is necessary. It will come to us, but it is only a stage on the journey and so becomes a breakthrough. So death is a gateway to glory.

Once, when visiting someone who was obviously dying,

I asked her if she was afraid. Obviously she feared pain, losing a grip on life, the loss of human dignity, she was afraid of the unknown. But what she feared most was being left completely alone. She said, 'Any pain is bearable'—I thought that a very brave statement—'but I fear being left completely alone'. Separation from others was more fearful than anything. This is still the hardest thing for many who are in hospital. It is not the approaching 'end', but the loneliness of the side-ward. I do not believe that we should leave people to face that 'great adventure' alone.

We are not alone. He is with us. Underneath are the everlasting arms—and those hands have the imprint of the nails. Right at the centre of the Christian faith is the Cross. There at the hub is a young man who has suffered injustice and all the hells that this world could hurl at Him. He is the scorned and rejected, and knows our sorrows.

With the dying person, I explored what Jesus suffered. It is amazing how much can be paralleled with what happens to us. He also had gone through it all, and triumphed. He is now alive and calls, 'Come to me'. One of the last, clear statements from that dear lady was, 'I do not know where I am going, or what will be there, but I know Who is coming to meet me'.

Here are lines from various Hebridean prayers:

Through Christ's crucifying tree,
Injury come not to me; . . .
Nor oppression may I see,
King of Glory leading me.

O thou Christ upon the tree,
All my hope I place in Thee.

May the cross of the crucifixion Tree
Where the wounded back of Christ we see,
Deliverance grant from distress to me,
From death, from spell-binding to keep me free.[3]

These are not charms against evil. They are affirmations that 'through the strength of His crucifixion and burial, we arise today'. The Cross loses its meaning if it is used like a charm to escape reality—or if it becomes so overlaid with gold and silver that it is only a thing of beauty. The Cross is the promise that God cares and is involved with us in all of life, and there is nowhere where He has not been. The Cross is the way to glory.

It was getting near home time and a storm had begun. One little lass had a long way to go down dark lanes. I worried for her and asked if I should go with her. She refused my help with a smile. 'There was no need, she would be all right, she was not afraid.' It was only at the last minute that I could relax, for her father arrived to take her home. She came over to me. 'I knew daddy was coming for me and he has brought me a new coat.' I watched them as they walked out the door together, she looked so radiant.

Much later I realised what a marvellous picture this was of the Christian facing death. We cannot avoid the storm or the dark, but we are not alone and we shall be given a 'new coat'. We may not know what lies ahead, but we know *Who*.

'Yea, though I walk through the valley of the shadow . . . I will fear no evil; for thou art with me.'[4]

EXERCISES

1. Know that He was crucified and lives, walks with you. Let Him walk into your past.

He walks into rooms that we thought locked indeed, that He may bring peace.

Experience that peace, His forgiveness and His living presence. He accepts you as you are.

Offer Him your failures and frustrations:
> all that you wish to forget,
> all that you cannot forgive,
> all that hurts and pains you.

Walk into areas that seem to be breaking down and know that He offers you His Presence, Resurrection and Life.

Know that *nothing* can separate us from the love of God in Christ Jesus.

2. Look at the sufferings of Jesus: Betrayal . . . desertion . . . denial . . . being alone . . . physical pain . . . a feeling of injustice . . . mockery . . . agony . . . death.
Find parallels in your own life. Know that in Him we are 'more than conquerors'.

3. *Another 5p.* Meditate on Psalm 23—'The Lord is my Shepherd.' Make an affirmation by reading very slowly, giving meaning to each word. The Lord *is* my Shepherd . . .
Then read Matthew 8.23-7.

Pause   Be still and know that He is God and that He is present . . . peace . . . etc . . .

Picture   A calm lake, beauty, a lovely place.
Allow a storm to hit it. A violent storm.
The waves are wild, the wind is fierce.
Trees are bending, branches breaking.
It gets dark. Things get worse.

Things are really out of control. *Chaos*.
Then . . .
A still small voice.
It pierces the storm and somehow triumphs over it.

Peace be still.
And there was a great calm.
Who would have believed it a minute ago?
It was like the end of the world . . . everything
doom and disaster and
now
the still waters.

Ponder   This is not a picture of a lake. It is my life.
Stormy, tempestuous, violent.
Strange, unpredictable winds blow.
Many a time we are in danger of sinking.
So many storms are because we 'go it alone'.
We do not call upon Him. And Jesus sleeps.

'O what peace we often forfeit,
O what needless pain we bear,
All because we do not carry
Everything to God in prayer.'

'Save us, Lord!' they said 'We are about to die!'
Wake Him.
Call upon Him.
Know that He is the Lord and Saviour.

Promise   To wake His Presence in my life.
To call upon Him in my need: 'To Thy Cross I look
and live.'
Affirm: 'With Jesus in my vessel I can smile amid
the storm.'

Prayer   'Lord Jesus, the sea is so large and our boat is so
small.'
'Lord, save us or we perish.'

I arise today
Through the strength of his death and burial.

'LET LOOSE
IN THE WORLD'

'Let Loose in the World'

I arise today
Through the strength of his resurrection with his ascension.

One cold grey day, I climbed up on to the high moors.
The game keepers were up there 'burning off' the heather,
and their fire attracted me. There was a great blaze. For
a while I just enjoyed the warmth and companionship.
The heather was perishing in the flames; it hissed as it
burned. These men knew what they were doing, all was
planned and under control. The area for 'burning off' had
been chosen carefully. The heather here had become old
and useless, all twisted and gnarled; it had lost its sweetness and no longer sustained the moorland life. So, it
perished in the flames. The game-keepers made sure the
peaty soil did not burn. After the fire, the earth would be
bare, blackened, lifeless. Then, one day, new shoots
would begin to show. The heather had not been
destroyed, only its old body. Under the peaty soil the
roots had been unharmed and soon sweet, life-sustaining
heather would grow once more. It had not perished, but
would arise, phoenix-like, from the flames.

Here for me was a picture of the Resurrection: the old
body may be destroyed, yet the essential being will not
perish, but have everlasting life. Watching the fire, I
looked forward to the new green shoots. An old French
tune came to mind and the words, 'Love is come again':

In the grave they laid him, Love whom men had slain,
Thinking that never he would wake again.
Laid in the earth, like grain that sleeps unseen:
Love is come again
Like wheat that springeth green.

Forth he came at Easter, like the risen grain
He that for three days in the grave had lain.
Quick from the dead my risen Lord is seen:
Love is come again
Like wheat that springeth green

When our hearts are wintry, grieving or in pain,
Thy touch can call us back to life again.
Fields of our hearts that dead and bare have been:
Love is come again
Like wheat that springeth green.[1]

Leaving the game-keepers and the 'burning off', I returned home strangely warmed, not by their fire, but by the Presence of the Risen Lord. There on the moor He had come again, and for me the day was no longer dull and grey.

In many ways the Celtic Church took the Resurrection for granted, because they experienced in their lives and worship the real Presence of the Risen Lord. There was no need for them to go back continually to the tomb and puzzle over it. They were not concerned about the empty tomb, they sought their Lord among the living. They took to heart the words of Scripture spoken to the followers of Jesus: 'Why are you looking among the dead for the one who is alive? He is not here; He has been raised'.[2]

Perhaps it is no accident that there was no appearance of Christ in the tomb. He does not want us to be held in that grey area, nor to concentrate our energies there. When we are faced with the Risen Lord, to spend our time looking into an empty grave is a foolishness. Christ the Risen Lord wants us to walk with Him in the fullness of life. He is not a theory about death and survival, He is a Person to be encountered, a Presence to meet. He is the Resurrection.

It is obvious that if we do not believe in the Resurrection, we cannot have met the Risen Lord. To *not* have met the Risen Lord leaves us with theories about life and death and problems about empty tombs. We are still the wrong side of Easter Day and so miss His glory. One of the old Irish commentators, writing on 1 Corinthians 15. 17, has said: 'It is manifest that unless you believe the Resurrection of Christ from among the dead, your faith will not sanctify you in that wise and will not save you from your sins.'

There is no doubt that the Resurrection is essential to our whole faith. Without His Resurrection, our faith becomes meaningless. If He is not raised, then there is no Resurrection or eternal life for us. Once we experience that He is risen, then life takes on a whole new meaning. We are no longer in the realm of theories; we are in eternal life. Patrick said in his *Confessions:*

> Without any doubt we shall rise on that day, in the clear shining of the sun, that is in the glory of Christ Jesus our Redeemer, as sons of the living God, and joint-heirs with Christ, and conformed to His image, that will be, since of Him and through Him and in Him we shall reign.

So already we begin to discover that we are the sons and daughters of God; we shall not perish but have everlasting life. We are learning that 'nothing shall separate us from the love of God'. Already we have inherited the Kingdom of Heaven.

Before the coming of Christianity, and long after the Irish talked of Tir-nan-Og 'the world of the Ever Young', this was already their feeling about life, that it could be eternal. This world was never far away, but ever close to them. This world could be stumbled upon by accident; you could be led into it by shining beings. It was there to be discovered, or seen by the mystic, though beyond the eyes of mortal men. It was this sort of feeling for eternity that made W.B.Yeats write: 'In Ireland this world and the world we go to after death are not far apart'.

It was not too difficult for the Celt to accept that 'the kingdom of heaven is at hand'. Nor was it too difficult to accept that if Christ is risen we should meet Him and let our lives intertwine. So in 'The Deer's Cry' Patrick could say:

Christ to shield me today . . .
Christ with me, Christ before me, Christ behind me.
Christ in me, Christ beneath me, Christ above me.
Christ on my right, Christ on my left,
Christ when I lie down . . . when I sit down . . . when I
arise.

Not only the Incarnate but the Risen Christ is there to be discovered. If you asked the Celt where is Jesus now, the reply would be very similar to the one Procula received from Longinus in Masefield's play, *The Trial of Jesus*. She asked, 'Do you think he is dead?' and he replied, 'No, lady, I don't.' When asked, 'Then where is he?' Longinus replied, 'Let loose in the world, lady.'

The Risen Christ is 'let loose in the world'. This discovery was first made in the greyness of the dawn by Mary Magdalene. For two nights she had not slept well. Her eyes were red with tears and lack of rest. She had seen Him die. It was as if evil had triumphed and injustice had won the day. How cruel this world is; and that is a fact. She had heard Him cry 'Why?' from the Cross, and it seemed there was no answer. She kept asking 'Why?' but it only made her more confused. There was not even an answer from God. A great heaviness settled on Mary's heart and mind, like the stone she saw rolled against the tomb. Such a weight! She wondered if anyone could lift it. If only someone would help, if someone would roll away the stone, she would go and be with Him. She might as well go to the grave, her hope and future were gone.

Before dawn came, Mary set off, still with the nagging question, 'Who will move the stone?' Who would move the heaviness in her heart and the great stone that sealed the grave? When she arrived in the garden, the stone was already rolled away. She knew it would take a lot of strength and courage to do that. Now she would go to her Lord. But He was not there. A grave robber must have been at work. She could hardly see for her tears, her vision was blurred. There was someone there in the garden; could it be the gardener? 'Sir, they have taken away my Lord. If you know where He is . . .' It was then that the stranger turned. 'Mary', he said. It was the Lord. He had robbed the grave and death and He is let loose in the world.

He is now to be met, to be discovered in our world. He can still be found in the garden, or on the seashore. The Resurrection stories will only make sense if we still experience and affirm His Presence as a reality.

A woman on the island of Harris was a leper, and so banished to the fringes of the island, to the seashore. In her treating of herself by the use of medicinal herbs and diet, she was healed. In thanksgiving, she rejoiced in the Presence of the Risen Lord:

> There is no plant in all the land
> But blooms replete with thy virtue,
> Each form in all the sweeping strand
> With joy replete thou dost endue,
>   O Jesu, Jesu, Jesu,
>   Unto whom all praise is due.[3]

This was not a lapse into a romantic pantheism, but a seeking of strength and solace from the Risen Lord. On Barra this was expressed even more strongly:

Jesus the Encompasser

Jesu! Only-begotten mine,
God the Father's Lamb sacrificed,
Thou didst give thy body's blood-wine
From the grave-death to buy me right.
My shield, my encircler, my Christ, my Christ!
For each day, each night, for each dark, each light;
My shield, my encircler, my Christ, my Christ!
For each day, each night, for each dark, each light.

Jesu! uphold me and be nigh,
My triumph, treasure, thou art now,
When I lie down, when stand, be by,
Whenever I watch, when I sleep.
My aid, my encircler, MacMary thou!
My strength everlasting, MacDavid, keep;
My aid, my encircler, MacMary thou!
My strength everlasting, MacDavid, keep.[4]

True strength and ability to triumph come from Him who has triumphed: 'through him, we have complete victory'.

Two people with their hopes shattered turned their backs on the Holy City. It was late in the day and they were on the road home to Emmaus. As they walked, they talked. It was then that He came, there on the ordinary road. He came as they journeyed and He walked with them. So He comes with us on our journey through life. We may not recognise Him, but He is present. We may not know what lies around the next corner, but it is our privilege to know Who it is Who goes with us.

The King to shield you in the glen,
The Christ to aid you on the ben,
Spirit to bathe you on the brae,
Hollow, or hill, or plain your way,
Be glen, or ben, or plain your way.[5]

When loved ones set out on a journey, to work at sea, or drive cattle overland, they are reminded of a Presence that never left them.

> Travelling the highland, travelling the townland.
>> Travelling the bogland long and wide,
> God the Son's herding round your hoofs' downland,
>> Safe and whole return home to bide,
> God the Son's herding round your hoofs' downland,
>> Safe and whole return home to bide.[6]

In the prayers of the Celts there are many journeying prayers that ask that we may know we are not alone, that He travels with us. Too many of us are like the travellers on the Emmaus road—our eyes are too dim to see Him. We need to learn to pray, 'Lord open my eyes, that I may see Thy risen Presence about me.'

Even though they did not recognise Him, the couple on arriving at Emmaus welcomed the 'stranger'. Here once more was the discovery that when we open our lives to the other, we give the Great Other the opportunity of coming in. At their table they made room for the unexpected guest, and there 'they recognised the Lord when he broke the bread.' A Grace before meals said on Benbecula runs:

> Be with me, O God, at breaking of bread,
> And be with me, O God, when I have fed.[7]

The Christ is still willing to sit at our table and share in our fellowship. He is still to be discovered in the 'breaking', if only we can open our eyes to His Presence. Unless Christ is at home in our home, we must really question our faith. For the Christian, faith is not a set of beliefs, but a relationship with the Risen Lord.

After a while, the disciples went fishing again on the Sea of Galilee; they returned to work. It was in that ordinary place, while they were working, that He appeared on the shore. Now He had been seen by individuals and groups; in the garden, on the road, at a meal in a living room, on the beach. Wherever they were, He came. No one returned to the tomb, for He had robbed it. They had no doubt that, whether they were in boat or barn, toiling or resting, their Lord went with them. They would naturally talk to Him, without any affectation ask Him to help them and to share their tasks. The Lord went with them and worked through them.

Too often we talk of Jesus as if He were a figure in history; we speak of what He did, what He has done, as if it were all over and finished with. We relegate Jesus to Palestine. But He is 'loose in the world'. With the Celt, we must learn to talk to Him rather than talk about Him. We must discipline ourselves so that we talk of Him in the present tense: 'Jesus is . . .' It is good to make statements and affirmations about Him in the present. Celebrate the Presence in the Present. For He is the Resurrection and He is here with us now. Today, I arise in the strength of His Resurrection.

The Ascension is the completing of the mission of Christ. He came down so that He could lift man up. He became man so that man could become Divine. The whole purpose of the Incarnation was to free us from the bonds of this world and lift us up to where He has gone before.

My favourite image of the Ascension comes from the earthly life of Jesus. Jesus is up in the mountains with the Father when a storm hits His disciples and threatens to engulf them. He comes down to where they are, to be with them in the storm. Somehow or other, though He is in the storm, He is above it. It does not swamp Him. He walks the waves. So He enters the storms and tempests of our lives. Peter is encouraged by the Presence and risks walking on the stormy water. For a while he appears to be able—it is amazing what we can achieve—but then, naturally, he begins to sink. Soon the storm will envelop him. Jesus does not let him sink into the depths; He will not let him perish. He reaches out His hand and raises him.

I know that Jesus still enters the storms of life. He comes down from the Father to lift us up. His hand raises us from that which would engulf us. When I am in the depths, I put my hand into the hand of the Risen and Ascended Lord. He lifts me out of the darkness into His own glorious light.

It was natural for the Celtic Christian to pray:

> 'Tis from my mouth that my prayer I say,
> 'Tis from my heart that my prayer I pray,
> 'Tis before thee that my prayer I lay,
> To thyself, O healing Hand, I call
> O thou Son of God who saves us all.
>
> O strengthen me in every good thing,
> In every strait thine encompassing,
> Safeguard me in every ill and pain,
> From every venom do thou restrain . . .
>
> Glorious master of star and cloud,
> Glorious Master of the sky browed,
> Glorious Master of heav'nly place.
> O blest by thee is each tribe and race.
>
> O mayest thou for me intercede
> With the great Lord of Life indeed.[8]

Because he believes in the real Presence at the close of the day, he asks for protection of the King of Heaven, that in the morning he may ascend. If by some mischance this night sleep should turn into death, he will still arise in the power of Christ.

I am going now into the sleep,
Be it that I in health shall wake;
If death be to me in deathly sleep,
Be it that in thine own arm's keep,
O God of grace, to new life I wake;
O be it in thy dear arm's keep,
O God of grace, that I shall awake!

Be my soul on thy right hand, O God,
O thou King of the heaven of heaven;
Thou it was who didst buy with thy blood,
Thine the life for my sake was given;
Encompass thou me this night, O God,
That no harm, no mischief be given.[9]

The message is clear and simple:

'Death is conquered. Man is free, Christ has won the Victory.'

EXERCISES

1. Make sure you talk of a living Lord in the present tense. Affirm: 'Jesus is . . . Jesus is alive . . . Jesus is here . . . Jesus is life . . . Jesus is . . .'

2. The Risen and Ascended Lord is present in your life. You cannot imagine it, but you can experience Him. Open your life to Him and let Him walk with you.

Walk with Him into the Past, into rooms of memory, and know that now He brings His love, His peace, His forgiveness. In the dark places today He shines. He comes to all those death-threatening events, in order that we should not perish. Amid the storms of passion He is there. Today, put your hand into the hand of God.

Walk with Him Today. This is what is most important. Do not leave Jesus in the past or in some distant future. He is here, saying, 'I will be with you always'. Invite Him into your daily life, share your journeys with Him. Let Him be there at the breaking of the bread (or the breaking of your heart). Let Him be at home in your home. Speak to Him freely and easily. Let it be seen that you have been (and are still) with Christ.

Walk with Him into the Future. Know that you never walk alone; He will not leave your nor forsake you. You may not know what lies ahead, but you know Who it is that goes with you. 'Lord Jesus, though I walk through the valley of the shadow of death, I will fear no evil: for Thou art with me.'

3. **Lord lift me**

> Lord, from this world's stormy sea
> Give your hand for lifting me
> Lord, lift me from the darkest night
> Lord, lift me into the realm of light
> Lord, lift me from this body's pain

Lord, lift me up and keep me sane
Lord, lift me from the things I dread
Lord, lift me from the living dead
Lord, lift me from the place I lie
Lord, lift me that I never die.[10]

I arise today,
In the strength of his resurrection with his ascension.

THE CHRIST
WHO COMES

The Christ who Comes

I arise today
Through the strength of his descent
for the judgement of Doom.

Throughout centuries of opposition and persecution, the Church never lost sight of the fact that God is in control. When it suffered and martyrs were made, the Church continued to rejoice: men and women triumphed under appalling conditions. There is story after story of their facing torture, and even death, with songs of praise in their hearts. At the extreme, some even courted martyrdom. Behind all, they were certain that God still cared and was in ultimate command, that He is a God of justice and will not let evil have the last word or triumph. What the writer to the Hebrews said of Moses applied to so many early Christians:

> He preferred to suffer with God's people rather than to enjoy sin for a little while. He reckoned that to suffer scorn for the Messiah was worth far more than all the treasures of Egypt, for he kept his eyes on the future reward.[1]

The day was coming when He would come again in His glorious majesty. Then all wrongs would be righted and the balance restored. Judgement was for sure: then He would welcome His own into His kingdom saying: 'Come, you that are blessed by my Father! Come and possess the kingdom which has been prepared for you ever since the creation of the world.'[2]

Like the early Church, the Celtic Church believed that this day of Judgement was imminent. St Patrick affirmed:

'We look for His coming soon as Judge of the quick and the dead.' In a hymn from the days of the Venerable Bede we have:

Suddenly to all appearing the great day of God shall
    come
As a thief at darkest midnight on an unsuspecting home:
Brief, indeed, shall all the glory of this age be seen to be,
When the world and all things in it shall have
    vanished visibly.[3]

'He will come again.' But if you ask, 'When?' the answer is not so simple. In a sense the answer is 'Now', for He will come again and again and again—He will come in the hungry and thirsty, in the prisoner and refugee. His coming is still a challenge. And still we are able to ignore Him. Still He 'comes to His own, but His own receive Him not'. Still He seeks entrance and is refused, He calls for aid in the desert and is left to die. He is the world's refugee. We continue to edge Him out of our world, out of our cities and fix Him on the Cross. Now, for us, is the day of judgement. 'Whenever you did this for the least of these, you did it for me.' Are you awake enough to recognise His coming, to hear His call? Would you see Him in a beggar needing a blanket for warmth, or as strangers knocking at your door? Is your home open enough to let Him in?

There is a terrible story of a black man who tried for many a month to get into a fashionable 'whites only' church and failed. In the end, in exasperation, he prayed to Christ and asked why it should be so. The reply from Christ was, 'I am not sure, for I have been trying to get in myself for years.' 'Whenever you did this for the least of these, you did it for me.' This is the Judgement. Today is the critical time. It is today that we are meeting Him. When the King comes in all His glory, it will not be the first time He has met us.

'Come ye blessed', He will say, 'and enter on the
 kingdom fair
By the Father's love prepared for you, ere the ages were;
Ye who with a brother's kindness succoured the
 distressed and the poor,
Rich with everlasting riches, reap love's guerdon
 evermore'.

So sang the Church in the days of Bede. The hymn continued:

Nor will the bitter sentence of the wicked long delay
The 'Depart from Me, ye cursed, from My Presence
 far away:
Me imploring aid and pity, have ye scornfully rejected:
Naked gave Me no clothing: sick and poor my woes
 neglected.'[4]

Because we did not recognise Him in the day of His coming, the most terrible words in all Scripture are pro-
nounced by the Christ in Majesty: 'I never knew you.'

It is because he comes continually that we are able to
meet Him, share with Him, converse with Him. Over the
years we get to know Him and He knows us, He becomes
our familiar friend. It is this living relationship that makes
any future Judgement far less threatening. We know Him,
we know His love and His forgiveness; He knows our
weaknesses and our need of Him. None of us knows
exactly what lies ahead for us, but we can know Who it is
who is there to meet us. Familiarity with our Lord Who
comes now, should take away fear of the future: 'Perfect
love drives out all fear'.

We do not fear death or Judgement, because He is with
us, though we do fear the unknown. The Celt prays:

Death that nor dread nor disgust conveys,
Death that nor terrifies or dismays.

> Dying the death of the saints on high,
> By me, my Soul-Physician, be nigh,
> The death of peace and tranquillity,
> Good the day grant thou to bury me.[5]

We look ahead with confidence, not in ourselves, but in our Lord.

> Since thou Christ by purchase the soul didst get—
> At the time when the life is paid away,
> At the time when bursts forth the body's sweat,
> At the time when up is offered the clay,
> At the time when away the blood is shed,
> At the time when the beam doth truly weigh,
> At the time when the upcaught breath is fled,
> At the time of the given judgement's say,
> Be the peace of the soul thine own to keep;
> Jesus Christ Son of Mary gentle Maid,
> Be the peace of the soul thine own to keep,
> O Jesu, in thine own keeping laid.[6]

It is through Him and in Him that we look ahead with hope.

His coming now, again and again, also means that we can prepare properly for that time when He will come in majesty. Even more important at the moment, it means we need not carry an unnecessary burden. He is the Lord to whom all hearts are open and from whom no secrets are hid, but He is also the Lord who says, 'Your sins are forgiven you.' Already we are able to begin to experience some of the joys of the kingdom. We can discover the great gift of forgiveness. It is amazing how many people are burdened with guilt or regret about some past event. The past is allowed to vibrate so strongly that it influences the present too much. We are unable to live well now because of what we have done and been. Each day we need to experience the fact of:

new perils past, new sins forgiven,
new thoughts of God, new hopes of heaven.

We can deny that we are sinners. We can pretend that we never live below par, but the Scripture is still true for everyone:

'If we say that we have no sin, we deceive ourselves, and there is no truth in us. But if we confess our sins to God, he will keep his promise . . . he will forgive us our sins and purify us from all our wrongdoing.'[7]

The Good News is that He is willing to forgive us if we are truly sorry. We need not be burdened with the past, but can walk in newness of life. Like the man carried by four and brought to Jesus, we can hear Him say: 'Your sins are forgiven . . . Get up and walk.'

The Church has seen regular confessions as a means to a healthier life now and as a preparation for the future. As Judgement is certain, the more slate we have clean the better. This is experienced in one of the poems from the Western Highlands:

Jesu, give unto me forgiveness of sin,
Jesu, be mine erring not forgotten within,
Jesu, give me the grace of repentance's school,
Jesu, give me the grace of forgiveness in full,
Jesu, give me the grace of submissiveness due,
Jesu, give me the grace of sincerity true,
Jesu, give me the grace of humility's part,
My confession to make at this time from my heart,
At throne of confession condemnation to own
Lest condemnation I find at the judgement throne;
Jesu, give me the strength and the courage, alone
At throne of confession condemnation to own
Lest condemnation I find at the judgement throne.
More easy is a season of chastening to me

Than a descent unto death for eternity.
Jesu, give unto me all my guilt to confess
With the urgency of death's importunateness.[8]

Confession and forgiveness gives opportunity for becoming free from the burden of sin. Knowing the Saviour and His love gives confidence in the Judgement. This does not avoid the facts of our sinfulness or that He will certainly come again to judge the living and the dead. Let us not become too confident, as the Church has from time to time, and heap up the blessings for ourselves and the curses for our enemies. There have been times in the history of the Church when she has gloated over the punishment of the wicked, almost taunted them that they may be condemned. That is far from a belief in a loving Saviour who prayed, 'Forgive them, Father! They don't know what they are doing.' But do let us be sure that Judgement is certain.

It is a pity that the Church seems to have stopped using the Advent season as a time to look at the 'Last Things'. We get so caught up with the tinsel of Christmas that we forget the challenges that the Christ in a manger presents. Some things are certain and ought to be faced: at least at some point in the church year and in the Church's teaching we should be made to face the ultimate realities. By tradition, the preaching in Advent was on the Four Last Things: Death, Judgement, Heaven and Hell. Only one of them can be avoided and it must be one of the last two!

The Church does a disservice to mankind if it omits Judgement from its gospel, or suggests that it will be all right for everyone. The gospel has always presented a challenge, and calls for decisions and actions. Our God is a just God and injustice cannot go on forever unchecked. This is not a stick to threaten a naughty child. This is one of the realities of life. Perhaps we are unable to look at these things today because we have lost that present awareness of Him who comes, and the future is full of threats. We should be able to see death as something as natural as falling asleep. It is not without cause that a saint's day of commemoration is not his birthday, but the day of his death, the day when he enters more fully into the glory that is to be revealed.

When at college, for a short while I helped to look after Father Stephen Bedale of the Society of the Sacred Mission in his last illness. It was obvious to him and to us all that he was soon to die. He had taught theology for years. When asked what he thought about his future his reply was, 'Soon I shall know whether all my theories were true.' Perhaps some of them were not, but he knew Who he was going to meet.

We should be able to walk out into the dark because we have put our hand into His, and to hear the familiar voice saying, 'It is I. Don't be afraid.' An Irish prayer of Recollection expresses such confidence in Him:

> Rule my thoughts and feelings
> You who brook no ill,
> Make me yours forever,
> Bend me to your will.
>
> Grant me Christ to reach you,
> With you let me be
> Who are not frail or fickle
> Nor feeble willed like me.[9]

It is because I know Him, and know He is a loving Saviour, that

I arise today,
Through the strength of his descent for the judgement
of Doom.

EXERCISES

1. Seek to be aware of 'Him who Comes'. When you watch or read the news, hear His call in the refugee, in the homeless and the unemployed. Look at your dealing with others and remember: 'Whenever you did this for the least of these, you did it for me.'

2.   Face—the realities that lie ahead.
    Death . . . Judgement . . . Heaven . . . Hell.
    Know that none of them need be faced alone or in fear.
    He who is the Judge is your loving Saviour and Friend.

3. Make your confession to Him each day. Talk over the day's events and seek His guidance and forgiveness. Remember that sin is not just the wrongs you have done, but the things you have left undone. One description of sin is living a life that fails to reach up to our potential; if it is through our own fault, we live below par.

> Lord,
> did I give a crown of thorn
> did I leave you all forlorn
> did I help to drive the nails
> did I run as courage fails
> did I tear you with the lance
> did I ever give you a chance?
> Was it I calling 'Crucify'
> or did I just pass you by?
> Have I sealed you in the tomb
> Have I lived a life of gloom
> Have I known you Risen King
> Have I let you change everything
> Have I seen the Judgement morn
> Have I let myself be reborn?

4. Think over the words of Bede: 'Christ is the day-star, who when the night of this world is past, promises and reveals to His saints, the eternal light of life.'

I arise today
Through the strength of his descent for the judgement of Doom.

68

THE COMMUNION
OF THE SAINTS

The Communion of the Saints

I arise today,
Through the strength of the love of the Cherubim,
In the obedience of angels,
In the service of archangels,
In the hope of the resurrection to meet with reward,
In prayers of patriarchs,
In prediction of prophets,
In preaching of apostles,
In faith of confessors,
In innocence of holy virgins,
In deeds of righteous men.

You can tell a man by the company he keeps. If a society is to be judged by its heroes, the generations that are being brought up on soap operas and television violence are in great danger. Today, children can sing television jingles almost as soon as they can talk, but the majority may never learn to sing a hymn of praise. Young folk know and relate to fantasy figures of the screen far better than they know or relate to God. In the mass of communications and the multi-choice of the media, a Presence is being lost from the earth. By turning on the TV at every moment of silence and every space in our lives, there is 'no room at the inn', no space for the Other to enter. Without that Presence, a glory has departed from the earth and life becomes a game of trivial pursuits. In his book *A Rumour of Angels* Peter Berger has suggested:

> A rediscovery of the supernatural will be, above all, a regaining of openness in our perception of reality . . . Perhaps more importantly, it will be an overcoming of

triviality. In openness to the signals of transcendence, the true proportions of our experience are rediscovered. This is the comic relief of redemption: it makes it possible for us to laugh and play with a new fullness.[1]

The Age of Reason, if based on reason alone, has been tested and found wanting. Once again we are extending our horizons and widening our perception of reality. The world has not changed much, nor the spirit of man. In old ways of expression, we can rediscover new depths in our lives. Francis Thompson tried to remind his generation that the 'Kingdom of God' was still with them and to be discovered. In a verse of the poem 'The Kingdom of God', he wrote:

> The angels keep their ancient places;–
> Turn but a stone, and start a wing!
> 'Tis ye, 'tis your estrangèd faces
> That miss the many-splendoured thing.

It is in the opening of our awareness that we begin to see all things anew. The author of the letter to the Hebrews extends our horizon when he says: 'Remember to welcome strangers in your homes. There were some who did that and welcomed angels without knowing it.'[2]

There is a story that St Cuthbert, when a young man, had such an experience at Ripon, where he was the guest-master of the Celtic monastery. One morning when the weather was wintry and snow lay on the ground, a visitor came for food and warmth. Cuthbert looked after him. He washed his guest's feet and rubbed them, on account of their being cold. He then left for a short while to get the man some food. When he returned, his guest had disappeared. Looking outside in the snow, there was no trace of footprints anywhere. On coming back inside, Cuthbert found three loaves of pure white flour awaiting him, and he gave thanks because the saying of the Lord was fulfilled:'He that receiveth you receiveth me, and he that receiveth me receiveth him that sent me.'[3] It is said that Cuthbert was visited by an angel.

The anonymous *Life of St Cuthbert* compares this story with that told in Genesis about Abraham in the Valley of Mamre.[4]

The sun was at its height. Abraham, as is the custom of the Bedouin, was resting in the shade of his tent opening, sheltered by the awning from the intense sun. Everything seemed to tremble in the haze; all seemed insubstantial as the heat rose from the sand. As he looked out, three shapes, hardly real, moved toward him. As they came closer, they became more substantial; the ethereal became three persons. This was no time to be out in the blazing sun. Abraham offered the strangers the hospitality of the desert, food to eat, something to drink. They had come a long way and had a message especially for him, a message from God. Once it was delivered, they rode off into the shimmering landscape, their shapes trembled and dissolved in the heat. They lost form and were gone. Who were they? Where had they come from? How ordinary were they? Abraham believed they were angels from God. Through them the transcendent had become immanent, the word had become flesh.

'Angel' is a Greek word that means messenger; most often it came to mean a messenger of God. The more we are aware of the Transcendent invading our world, the more we become aware of angels, of bearers of His messages. That messenger can take many forms, but is still an angel. In *The Early Life of Patrick* by Muirchu it is said of him:

The angel was wont to come to him on every seventh day of the week; and as one man talks to another, so

Patrick enjoyed the angel's conversation. Moreover in the sixteenth year of his age, he was taken captive, and for six years he was a slave, and throughout thirty changes of service, the angel used to come to him; and he enjoyed angelic counsel and conversation.[5]

Muirchu identifies this angelic visitor as one named Victor, who often visited Patrick. In his own account of his call back to Ireland Patrick wrote:

I saw in the night visions a man whose name was Victorious, come as it were from Ireland with countless letters. And he gave me one of them and I read the beginning of the letter which was entitled 'The Voice of the Irish'.[6]

It was Patrick's awareness of the message from Victor that made Victor an 'angel'. In the Outer Hebrides the word *Comain*, which means 'companion' or 'friend' is sometimes used to mean 'angel'. If our vision was extended a little, we would begin to see angels among our visitors and companions. This is not just a way of talking but a way of experiencing the Transcendent.

Bede complained about the Celtic Church's love for story. What he failed to see was the desire for the heroic, and to view life as an adventure. Our choice of heroes helps not only to show our character, but in time to affect our character and way of thinking. We all look for stories and heroes that give meaning to life or triumph over it. If we choose men of violence, or the modern anti-hero, we should not be surprised that the elements they exemplify appear in our life—and that they grow. The proliferation of violence and sexual perversions on stage and screen does not help, but probably far worse is the sheer trivialisation of so much of life, which almost stops us from reacting to anything. We are able to recite names and exploits of our favourite screen characters; how many saints do we know anything about? We can report television advertisements; how many prayers do we know by heart? Again, we are in danger of missing out on the 'many-splendoured thing'.

For the Celtic Church it was a very thin line that divides the saints triumphant from us on earth. Those who witnessed before us and are received up into glory are very much alive. They are not men and women of the past, but sons and daughters of God, who are alive now and in the fullness of eternal life. The Communion of the Saints is a reality to be experienced. Often the Celt would choose one of the saints for his 'soul friend'. He would converse with him and ask him to pray for him. The Supplication of the Saints became as natural as talking to a friend on earth and asking him to pray for you. The Celt would say:

> I pray and supplicate
> Cuibh and Columba,
> The Mother of my King,
> Brigit womanly,
> Michael militant,
> High-King of the angels,
> To succour and shield me.[7]

This was not a prayer of empty words, but addressed to people who were known through story, prayer and legend, whose presence was still allowed to vibrate on the earth. If we do not know of the saints and their deeds, then this part of our perception is diminished.

One of the ways of testing our vision of life is to compare it with the vision of others. Remember, a nation without a vision perishes; this is just as true for individuals. We all need a vision of who we are and where we are going, or we shall stumble and be completely lost. Once I learned (from I don't know where):

75

A man with work and no vision is a slave
A man with vision and no work is a dreamer
A man with vision and work is a prophet.

By looking at the lives of men and women who have tri-umphed, by discovering what gave their lives meaning and purpose, we can see pointers for ourselves. The reading of rich lives certainly enriches us. A good idea is to obtain a book on the saints that tells you about the saint for the day and about his or her love for God and vision of life. Spend a little time trying to see what it meant for them and consider if it can mean anything for you.

I often think the mind is like a video-tape that cannot easily be wiped clean. Everything you have ever done, read or experienced is on this tape for good or ill; all the rich and life-giving experiences and all the impoverishing and destructive ones. Much of our life we are able to keep in control, and select from that video what we want. But not always. There are times when the video seems set on random selection, and it turns on to all sorts of things. There are times when I go to church to pray, I kneel before the altar and then instead of prayer, I battle with some of the wickedest thoughts of the week. Because I have stopped busying myself, the mind switches from being fixed in certain tight channels to being free. This experience is by no means rare or new. From an early Celtic monastery comes 'A Prayer for Recollection':

> How my thoughts betray me!
> How they flit and stray!
> Well they may appal me
> On great judgement day.
>
> Through the psalms they wander
> Roads that are not right,

Mitching, shouting, squabbling
In God's very sight;

Through august assemblies,
Groups of gamesome girls,
Then through woods, through cities
Like the wind in whirls . . .

Lost to recollection
Near and far they roam,
From some monstrous errand
Slyly they slink home.[8]

We all have minds that are hard to control! But ways have
been discovered of helping to keep us reasonably on the
right tracks. If the mind records everything we experience, we should be careful what we record on it. We can
to some extent choose. There will always be a mixture of
good and evil, of life and destruction, but we can influence
the mixture by deliberate choice. Quite often, our attitude
to what we do will influence our attitude in the future. It
is with this insight that the writer to the Philippians says:

May you always be joyful in your union with the Lord.
I say it again: rejoice! Show a gentle attitude towards
everyone. The Lord is coming soon. Don't worry about
anything, but in all your prayers ask God for what you
need, always asking him with a thankful heart. And
God's peace, which is far beyond human understanding, will keep your hearts and minds safe in union with
Christ Jesus.

In conclusion, my brothers, fill your minds with
those things that are good and that deserve praise:
things that are true, noble, right, pure, lovely, and
honourable . . . And the God who gives us peace will
be with you.[9]

This deliberate choice can be called Meditation. It happens when we choose certain things and dwell on them. Because we all meditate on things, we should learn to meditate well and discover thought-patterns that work well for us. Once again we can turn to the lives of the saints for help—we can learn from those who have tested certain methods and have shown that they work for the good of mankind. We should see in the saints men and women of expertise, and learn from their dedication and example. To ignore the great and noble figures from our past is to rob the present of much treasure; even worse, it is to fail to realise the potential of the Communion of the Saints. It is when we have discovered these heroic men and women, when our vision has widened and our sensitivity extended, that we can say with greater meaning:

Therefore with angels and archangels, and with all the company of heaven, we laud and magnify thy glorious name; evermore praising thee, and saying,

Holy, holy, holy, Lord God of hosts, heaven and earth are full of thy glory. Glory be to thee, O Lord most High.[10]

EXERCISES

1. Find a book of Saints laid out with dates throughout the year. Use it daily and seek to discover what made these men and women able to triumph.

> Fill our lives, O Lord, with
> The Alleluias of Angels,
> The Hosannas of Heaven,
> The Perception of Prophets,
> The Awareness of Apostles,
> The Faith of our Fathers,
> The Courage of Confessors,
> The Eagerness of Evangelists,
> The Diligence of Disciples,
> The Directness of Doctors,
> The Praise of Priests,
> The Mightiness of Martyrs,
> The Virtue of Virgins,
> and the Steadfastness of Saints.

2. Learn by heart the prayers of the Saints. Prayers like 'The Deer's Cry', or the prayer of St Francis of Assisi:

> Lord, make me an instrument of your peace;
> Where there is hatred, let me sow love,
> Where there is injury, pardon,
> Where there is discord, union,
> Where there is doubt, faith,
> Where there is sadness, joy.
> O Divine Master,
> Grant that I may not so much seek
> To be consoled as to console,
> To be understood as to understand,
> To be loved as to love.
> For it is in giving that we receive,
> It is in pardoning that we are pardoned,
> And it is in dying that we are born to Eternal life.

Learn the prayers that have special meaning for you. Not to have a store of prayer is to rob ourselves of our heritage.

3. Learn to Meditate.
Read again Philippians 4.4–8.
The mind can be compared to a pool of very muddy water. You cannot get rid of the dirt, but you can let it settle to the bottom of the pool. Each day, drop into the pool clear drops of water . . . the good . . . the lovely . . . the true . . . the holy. Make sure that more clear water is added each day. Take your time to do it. In times of trouble and stress there is no doubt that the dirt will be churned up from the bottom, but the more clear water you have dropped into the pool, the less dirty it is able to become. Make sure that what you concentrate on is for your good and can be offered to the glory of God.

> *I bind unto myself the power*
> *Of the great love of the Cherubim;*
> *The sweet 'Well done' in judgement hour;*
> *The service of the Seraphim,*
> *Confessors' faith, Apostles' word,*
> *The Patriarchs' prayers, the Prophets' scrolls.*
> *All good deeds done unto the Lord,*
> *And purity of virgin souls.*

THE EARTH
IS THE LORD'S

The Earth is the Lord's

I arise today
Through the strength of heaven:
Light of sun,
Radiance of moon,
Splendour of fire,
Speed of lightning,
Swiftness of wind,
Depth of sea,
Stability of earth,
Firmness of rock.

One of the saddest impressions that some Christians give is that they do not love this beautiful world: they do not thrill to its ordering or its mysteries. Let us show beyond doubt that we believe this is God's world, we believe in a Creator, and that every part of this world ought to show that it belongs to Him: He made it all. It is in this world that He has chosen to create us; we are here to live to His glory. If we do not enjoy this world, it must be because something has spoiled it, or that we do not approve of His handiwork. It is in this world that God has set us a task, and chosen to reveal Himself to us. If we are not at home in the only world that He gives to us, why should we believe we would be satisfied with another?

This world is not only His creation, but He loves it. He did not make it because He despises it or wants to destroy it, He loves it as His own; so much so that because it has been marred, He gave Himself to redeem it. He became Incarnate, and came down to earth. He asks us to do the same, to come down to earth. Perhaps it is no accident that *humus* and *humility* are words that are close in our language. It is the person who involves himself with the humus, who is not afraid of being down to earth, who will experience the exaltation of the Presence. It is therefore terribly perverse for Christians to become 'so heavenly-minded that they are no earthly good'. It is this precious globe that is our home for the time being, and here He is to be found.

When I read what Matthew Arnold wrote of the Carthusian monks:

> Wandering between two worlds, one dead
> The other powerless to be born,
> With nowhere yet to rest my head.[1]

I want to shout, 'No, not so.' Perhaps Matthew Arnold was just expressing his own being out of tune. When we are out of touch with the world, we should never blame God, for He never loses contact with it. The fault 'lies not in the stars but in ourselves'.

There is hardly a country in the world that has expressed such a love for nature as Ireland. In the early centuries of the Christian era, the love for nature expressed by the Celts was quite unique. Even toward the end of his life when Columba had achieved so much, he longed for beautiful Derry:

> Were all the tribute of Scotia mine
> From its midland to its borders,
> I would give it all for one little cell
> In my beautiful Derry.[2]

I am fortunate in living in a beautiful moorland area with clear streams and purple heather. Part of my parish has a village that used to be called Colman Argos, the little shieling of Colman. Legend says that after the Celtic Church lost its case at the Synod of Whitby in 664, Bishop Colman rested here and built a little shieling before returning to Ireland. Legend also attributes these thoughts to Bishop Colman:

> I wish, O Son of the living God,
> O Ancient, Eternal King,
> For a little shieling in the wilderness,
> That there may be my dwelling;
> A lithe grey lark to be by its side,
> A clear pool to wash away my sins.[3]

Not a place to escape from the world, but where he could immerse himself more deeply in it, and have time to converse with its Creator. We may not be able to live in such a place, but at least we can create one in our heart; a little shieling where we can meet our Maker. This is often the way to discover that God is also in the factory and in the city street. Once Moses had found the burning bush, he knew that God was there in desert as well as in palace.

> Earth is crammed with heaven
> And every common bush afire with God,
> But only he who sees, takes off his shoes.[4]

I sometimes like to reverse that last line to say, 'He who takes off his shoes sees'. It is often through a respect for nature and a seeking out of its mysteries that we discover the Mystery to be enjoyed.

There has to come a day for each of us, when we wake to the fact that 'the place on which you stand is Holy Ground.' It is in the absolutely ordinary parts of life that He comes to meet us. Like the prodigal son, we may have chosen to live in 'a far-off country', but if we turn around, He meets us on the road. The call to repentance is not just about sorrow for evil deeds, but a call to those who have taken the wrong path. 'Repent' means 'Turn around and see. You have been looking the wrong way; the kingdom of heaven is at hand.' The discovery that God encompasses us on every side is, for many, a joyful homecoming—to be at home in the Earth where we belong. To discover that God waits for us in creation, and in fact comes along the road to meet us.

One day I went out into the garden to cut a few flowers for the table. The dew was still on the grass and the world had an early morning freshness. I made for a bed of peony roses, to pick a few. The very first flower seized my whole attention. I realised that I had never looked at this flower before: I had not noticed how many different reds were in its petals, I had not felt the firmness of its stem, nor the velvetness of its flower. What a strange centre it had to it! I wanted to look deeper. Little bits of information came to mind. I had read somewhere that its roots were used to cure palsy, and that it was used against storm and tempest. But where had this flower come from? Where did the first peony come from, the first flower? I could trace its family tree back and back in history until I became lost in time. What then? I could spend hours and hours on this 'problem' and enjoy it; days trying to work it out, sleepless nights trying to solve it. But the flower was here and now and presenting itself to me in all its beauty. There it stood with the mystery of life in it, and many of the mysteries of the universe; and it had presented itself to me. I was captured for a while by this 'mystery to be enjoyed'. But even more, under my very gaze, a Presence had invaded my little world. The only thing that had kept Him out until this moment had been my inability to see Him. Now 'the Lord is in this place', and I knew it. How appropriate that in German this flower is called *Pfingstenrose*—Whitsun rose— time when the Presence was revealed in all His fullness to the apostles.

The mystical union is no sweet romanticism, though it may sound like that when put into words. It is not so much a way of running from reality as of entering much more deeply into it. So often we glide over the surface of

86

things and experiences, when the very depths can be ours. It is important to strive to see things as they really are, in depth and in intensity. We live in a wonderful world where every bit of matter influences another. Great forces are at work in sun and moon, light, tides and seasons. We live with plants and trees and flowers every bit as much as we live with roads and streets and crowds. If we truly want to live to the full, we need to overcome our insensitivity to what is around us. It is worth taking ordinary things of our day-to-day life and developing our awareness. Who knows, even in our hands, a little soil might still be able to open the eyes of the blind. In *Le Milieu Divin*, Teilhard de Chardin says that God:

> 'is not far away from us, altogether apart from the world we see, touch, hear, smell and taste about us. Rather he awaits us at every instant in our action, in the work of the moment. There is a sense in which he is at the tip of my pen, my spade, my brush, my needle—of my heart and of my thought . . . by virtue of Creation and still more of Incarnation, *nothing* here below is *profane* for those who know how to see. On the contrary everything is sacred . . .[5]

It is with this heart and mind that I seek to look at the Universe. Everything we see and do should be done with adoration. It is not that we are too involved with creation, it is that we have not allowed ourselves to be involved enough. Christianity is not a forsaking of the world, but that which gives it more meaning and purpose; it helps us to be at home in our Father's house. In typical Gallic fashion de Chardin says:

> We have only had to go a little beyond the frontier of sensible appearances in order to see the divine welling through . . . By means of all created things, without

exception, the divine assails us, penetrates us, and moulds us. We imagined it as distant and inaccessible, whereas we live steeped in its burning layers. *In eo vivimus*. As Jacob said, awakening from his dream, the world, this palpable world, which we were wont to treat with the boredom and disrespect with which we regard places with no sacred association for us, is in truth a holy place, and we did not know it. *Venite adoremus*.[6]

Many in the Celtic Church were blessed in discovering, almost naturally, that if you are in touch with creation, then you are in touch with its Creator. But if our attitude to creation is wrong, then our attitude to our Creator will also be wrong. Much of our insensitivity to the world, our misuse of its resources, our destruction of great areas, is because we have lost awareness of the mysteries and the strange bonds that link all things. Those who only use the world for what they can get out of it have lost touch with its Creator.

For the Celt there was not a part of the earth, or of the day, that should be free from adoration or consecration. It would begin on rising with prayers of dressing. Already we have imagined Patrick lacing up his tunic and saying:

> *I bind unto myself today*
> *The strong name of the Trinity . . .*

beginning the morning by expressing his belief in and calling upon the Sacred Three. Then, before his journey and whilst fastening his leggings, he would say:

> *I bind unto myself today*
> *The power of God to hold and lead,*
> *His eye to watch, his might to stay,*
> *His ear to hearken to my need.*

Every event is sacred and affirms the Presence. At fire-lighting:

This morning I will kindle fire upon my hearth
Before the holy angels who stand about my path,
Both Ariel the lovely and Uriel of grace,
Beneath the sun not frightened by one of human race,
No envy, hatred, malice, no fear upon my face,
But the Holy Son of God the guardian of the place.[7]

Such really earthy prayers, like 'Milking Prayer':

> Be blessing, O God, my little cow,
> And be blessing, O God, my intent;
> O God, my partnership blessing thou,
> And my hands that to milking are sent.
>
> Be blessing, O God, each teat of four,
> Be blessing, O God, each finger's pull;
> Be blessing thou each drop that doth pour
> Until, O God, my pitcher be full![8]

There are prayers for churning the milk for butter, for weaving, cattle driving, journeying, sailing; there are prayers for every part of life. Nothing is seen to be outside the encompassing Presence of God. It is our own dullness and blindness that stops us seeing that all of life is consecrated. We need to learn to look deeper and discover again that 'in Him we live and move and have our being'. Sacredness is indigenous. It is there by right of being part of His world. For me, this is expressed in the Reaping Prayer from South Uist:

> O God, thyself my reaping bless,
> Each ridge, and meadow, mossy-field,
> Each sickle's hard curved shapeliness,
> Each ear and binding of the yield,
>   Each ear and binding of the yield.
>
> Each maiden bless, each youth so slight,
> Women and tender young ones all,
> Mark them beneath thy shield of might,

And guard them in the saints' wide hall,
    And guard them in the saints' wide hall.

Each goat, each little lamb, each sheep,
Each cow and horse and barnstore-hold,
The flocks and herds, surrounding keep,
And tend them to a kindly fold,
    And tend them to a kindly fold.[9]

We need to tune again the 'five-stringed harp'. Awaken to the Presence.

One of the ways in which I seek to do this is to meditate on created things. Every week I take something in my hands and seek to allow its presence to speak. In the words of William Blake:

To see a World in a Grain of Sand,
And a Heaven in a Wild Flower,
Hold Infinity in the palm of your hand,
And Eternity in an hour.[10]

Once or twice every week I do not meditate on the Bible, but take as my text something of earth: I seek to discover the mysteries of creation. I take a stone and meditate on that, or a flower, or an apple. I have learned to meditate on sun, moon and stars, on basic elements like light, water, air and soil. Here, not only is my relationship with the world deepened; I have learned a lot more respect and sensitivity towards fellow creatures. I have learned great mysteries that are there and to be enjoyed. I have been discovered by the Presence.

I believe that choosing earthy things as a 'text' and meditating on them is something we are all capable of. As an example, at school we were talking about the desert and the need for water. It was not long before we were looking at water itself and its creation. From this arose this little meditation:

One upon a time, before time itself, before the sun shone for a day and the moon told of the night, while you were part of a great star and a spirit in ether, there was a Big Bang. It was so big that if you had ears they would have burst. The Bang was so big it would have killed anything alive, but there was nothing living.

In that Bang, pieces of a great star were spread over millions and millions of miles, each bit burning bright; so hot their fires would burn for millions of years. Even today the sun burns with that fire and inside the earth the fire stirs up now and again. Only the moon has let its fire go out, so now it borrows light from the sun.

The earth was a flaming ball. The fire burned not for a night, not for a week, but for years and years and nothing could live. From the fire rose great clouds of smoke: mighty clouds, miles deep, and they went right around the world. They cut out the sun, they blocked out the light and the earth felt a change. Maybe it was a little cooler.

In the dark clouds gases met together, united, and a little drop of rain was born. The first drop of rain ever to come towards the earth—but it sizzled up before it arrived and turned to gases again. Soon it was there again with brothers and sisters. Not one drop, but a hundred, and again the fires burned them up. Soon their family was getting bigger. The next time they came, they landed and put out a little of the fire. Now a battle began—fire and water fought. It began to rain— not for a day, not for a week, but for hundreds and thousands of years. Parts of the earth became cool. The raindrops made their home here. They became streams and rivers and mighty seas. In most areas, the fire hid underground and awaited its time. The black smoke clouds disappeared. The rain stopped falling, the sun shone, the seas reflected its light and waited for life.

God had made the earth.

EXERCISES

1. Learn to rejoice in creation. Once or twice a week, take some created thing and seek to look at it in depth, to discover its mystery. An alternative way is, each day of the week, to explore and give thanks for another piece of creation, perhaps following the order of Genesis 1.

Monday: Explore the beginnings; order out of chaos, light out of dark.

Tuesday: Rejoice in sky, cloud and air.

Wednesday: Discover the riches of water, the depths of the seas, of ice and snow. Rejoice in stream and river.

Thursday: Wonder at the sun and moon and stars of light. Explore the mysteries of the galaxies, day and night, tides and seasons.

Friday: Rejoice in all living things, plants, fish, birds and animals. Learn of their variety, individuality.

Saturday: Enjoy your own humanity. Explore the wonders of human life. Treat others with awe and deep respect.

Sunday: Rejoice in the Presence that abides in all things, and rest in Him.

2. Seek to become more aware of the 'Glory'

> Awaken us to your glory
> Dispel the darkness of night
> Destroy the heaviness of heart
> Cure the blindness of sight
> Heal the deafness of ears
> Open the mouth that is dumb
> Restore a gentleness of touch
> Encourage a sense of adventure
> Bring an awareness of You
> Awaken us to Your Glory.

Let us not live out of tune with creation.

3. Remember that you are part of creation and give thanks for that fact. Perhaps you could use the Hymn of St Francis:

O Most High Almighty good Lord God: to Thee belong
    praise, glory, honour and blessing.
Praised be my Lord God with all His creatures, and especially
    for our brother the sun who brings us the day and who
    brings us the light.
Fair is he and shines with very great splendour.
O Lord, he signifies to us Thee.
Praised be my Lord for our sister the moon: and for the stars,
    the which he has set clear and lovely in the heaven.
Praised be my Lord for our brother the wind: and for air and
    cloud, calms and all weather by which Thou upholdest in
    life all creatures.
Praised be my Lord for our sister water: who is very
    serviceable unto us, and humble, precious, clean.
Praised be my Lord, for our brother fire, through whom Thou
    givest us light in darkness; he is bright, pleasant, very
    mighty and strong.
Praised be my Lord for our mother the earth, which doth
    sustain us and keep us: and brings forth divers fruits and
    flowers of many colours and grass.
Praised be my Lord for all those who pardon one another for
    His love's sake; and who endure weakness and tribulation.
Blessed are they who shall peaceably endure: for Thou O Most
    Highest shall give them a crown.
Praised be my Lord for our sister death of the body: blessed
    are they who are found walking by Thy holy will.
Praise ye and bless ye the Lord and give thanks unto Him and
    serve Him with great humility. Alleluia. Alleluia.

(As an alternative to this translation, you can use the hymn
   'All Creatures of our God and King'.)

> *I bind unto myself today*
> *The virtues of the starlit heaven,*
> *The glorious sun's life-giving ray,*
> *The whiteness of the moon at even,*

The flashing of the lightning free,
The whirling wind's tempestuous shocks
The stable earth, the deep salt sea,
Around the old eternal rocks.

THE PRESENCE
OF GOD

The Presence of God

I arise today
Through God's strength to pilot me:
God's might to uphold me,
God's wisdom to guide me,
God's eye to look before me,
God's ear to hear me,
God's word to speak to me,
God's hand to guard me,
God's way to lie before me,
God's shield to protect me,
God's host to save me
From the snares of devils,
From temptation of vices,
From every one who shall wish me ill,
Afar and anear,
Alone and in a multitude.

As St Patrick prepared himself for the conflict that lay ahead, he put his faith in the Divine Reality. He was not alone in his battle, for the Almighty was with him—the Father was there to uphold, guide and protect. Patrick was sure it was God's path that lay before him and God's strength that was given to him.

When we turn to the Celtic Church, we discover men and women who are quite simple, are not particularly clever or gifted, but to them, God is a living and glorious reality which supernaturalises their everyday life and transforms their most ordinary events into sublime worship. For them God is not of the past, or confined to the Bible and the Holy Land, but the Divine Reality to be encountered each day, in each event and each decision.

This is a God of the now, involved in the present situation, and His will and way are to be discovered and followed. We arise today in the Divine Presence—and that is reality. When we lose sight of this, we enter the realms of fantasy. Losing sight of God makes us believe in our own strength and wisdom, believe we are self-sufficient and able to cope. But if we dare to stop to think, we know this is not so. Without God there is nothing we can call eternal, and we are certainly perishable goods. It is not our ideas of God, our feelings about Him, but His Presence that is Divine Reality.

Inside the Bible which I use every day is a pressed flower. It is there as a reminder. Every now and again when I turn to it, I remember a pleasant summer's day with friends at an old mill. With effort I can recall the laughter and the love. Time has made it sound more glorious. When I am not at ease in the present, nostalgia is an escape. Even now, memories vibrate. But the event is gone, the flower has faded. Pressed out, the flower has lost much; it no longer smells, its stem is very fragile and brittle. It has been changed in the pressing between the pages, and has lost much of its original vitality.

Experiences cannot be captured and pressed into pages of books or reports without losing much of their vitality. Once we try to put them into words, or to preserve them in any way, change takes place. Too often we attempt to write down an experience because we have already lost it. Words cannot replace the reality any more than a photograph can make up for a lost presence. So much that we experience cannot be tied down or captured in any way.

If this is true of our everyday life, how much more so is it of the Divine Reality? No matter how hard we try, we cannot press God into the pages of a book. Even the Bible cannot contain Him, and is a poor substitute for the Real Presence. What we read is useful so long as it makes certain things vibrate in our lives. But we need the 'Word made flesh', the awareness that He dwells among us. Salvation is not of the Bible. It is of God. When battles are to be fought, or decisions made, the Word we need is the Presence. We do not take a book, but rather turn to a Companion.

It is good to remember that not only books, but theologians and preachers also, cannot comprehend God. He cannot be contained within their theories and systems. He forever breaks free. St Augustine of Hippo recognised this when he attempted to put his experiences of the Trinity into words. He compared his efforts to those of a little child busy on the beach. The boy was running from the sea with small quantities of water, trying to fill a hole in the sand. The sea was never any the less and the hole never really filled. So futile are our attempts at comprehending God with our intellect.

Every time we try to reduce God to our comprehension, we make Him too small. We try to press the Infinite into a very minute, finite area. Yet for many, God is little more than a theory about life, something we have been taught. It is especially sad to meet intelligent people who have not developed beyond a Sunday School understanding of God. If we allow God to become a fixed idea, one theory among many, we relegate Him to the gods. Once we have a static god, we have not only an idol, but a god who dies. If we allow our God to become an idea, rather than a companion, then we are likely to experience the death of god—if such a god ever lived. But let us be aware that that does not affect the Divine Reality. Our ideas may die, but He is still present though we are unaware.

One way to view the crucifixion is to see it as an attempt by man to fix God. Man seeks to edge God out of his daily life and routine, out of the city and into a fixed position. Man chooses to have a god who does not 'interfere'. The crucifixion begins when we limit God to our way of thinking and our wills and desires. We often act as if it were our duty to chaperone God! But God, so fastened, refuses to be bound. Nails and graves will not hold him, only love. So the writer of *The Cloud of Unknowing* says:

> He cannot be comprehended by our intellect, or any man's—or any angel's for that matter. For both they and we are created beings. But only to our intellect is He incomprehensible, not to our love.[1]

He repeats this thought a little later when he says: 'By love he can be caught and held, but by thinking, never.'[2]

We need to discover that the prayers of the saints are affairs of the heart. Too many have tried to fix the Beloved rather than risk the adventure of courting Him and being courted by Him. If He is fixed, we shall be unable to venture. Like Moses, we shall say, 'If you do not go with us, we will not go'. But if we journey with the Beloved, we have a new heart for our travels. Often when the Scriptures seem dull, and prayers fail to vibrate, it is because our love has grown cold—either we have ignored Him and so got out of tune, or we have exchanged the Living Presence for 'pressed flowers'. Let us remember that creeds cannot satisfy our innermost longings, nor can any book, only a personal experience of Him in whom we live and move and have our being.

As part of our daily prayers we need to bind ourselves to Him in love, knowing that He already loves us. Part of our daily routine should be to 'practise the Presence of God', calling upon Him, knowing that He is more ready to hear than we are to pray. To do this, we will need to discipline our lives. We will need to learn a stillness that allows God to work instead of us. If only we would make room, God is willing to enter. We need to shut out those things that prevent us from loving Him and expressing His love, and make ourselves quiet for His coming:

> I weave a silence on to my lips
> I weave a silence into my mind
> I weave a silence within my heart
> I close my ears to distractions
> I close my eyes to attractions
> I close my heart to temptations.
>
> Calm me O Lord as you stilled the storm
> Still me O Lord, keep me from harm
> Let all tumult within me cease
> Enfold me Lord in your peace.[3]

Once we have quietened ourselves, it is good to affirm the Presence, to assure ourselves of the reality that we have lost sight of: 'Nothing can separate us from the love of God'. No matter what storm rages about us, or who is against us, we are still 'in heavenly love abiding'. I know this is true, but I need to tell it to myself again and again. One of the ways of doing this is to use our whole being to proclaim His Presence: God in our lips, God in our minds, God in our hearts, God in reality.

> 'Tis from my mouth that my prayer I say,
> 'Tis from my heart that my prayer I pray,
> 'Tis before thee that my prayer I lay,
> To thyself, O healing Hand, I call
> O Thou Son of God who saves us all.[4]

We need to discipline ourselves to this proclamation: 'God in our lips'. Use your *mouth* to proclaim His Presence and Power. Let it be heard by yourself and by others:

> I believe, O God of all gods, that you are
> The Eternal Father of Life.[5]

State clearly that you believe in a God who is present.

Vary the attribute that you ascribe to God according to your need at the time: The Eternal God of Love . . . Peace . . . Joy . . . Repeat the sentence you choose and now bring your *mind* into action. Make sure that you understand what you are saying. Emphasise *His* Eternal Presence—the fact that it is *God* and that He is. Then you can add the attributes that God brings to your need and know that He is able. Visualise God supplying what you lack.

Now open your *heart* to Him. Know that all is only possible because of His love for you. He cannot be contained in books, but will be found in your heart. He is too great to be grasped, but will be held by love. He gives His resources to you because He gives Himself.

Rest, knowing that it is all possible, not because of your words, thoughts or love, but because of His Love and Presence. This is the Reality offered: here, at this very moment, God in mouth, in mind, in heart, in reality. No matter how feeble your efforts, He is still there and ready to meet your needs.

One of the dangers of this way of praying is that we can come with ulterior motives. We come not for His Presence but His presents. We come for what we can get out of Him, the gifts He gives us. Rather than seeking God, we come seeking peace, or love, or healing, or some other attribute. If we are given the gift, there is a danger that we will ignore the Giver.

There are lots of techniques which help us towards inner calm or to achieve more out of life. There are various disciplines that will improve our control of body, mind and even spirit. Such training helps us to discover our potential and to realise our abilities, and for that reason should be welcomed and encouraged. Every improvement in our attitude and life should be accepted as good. But after all of this we should remember we are not self-sufficient, nor are we almighty. For us all, there will come a time when 'we have no power of ourselves to help ourselves'. Let us face the fact that in our own right we are perishable beings. 'We are not sufficient in ourselves to help ourselves—our sufficiency is of God.' The gifts of life, health, strength, peace and wisdom are not everlasting—unless they are of God. We need the Presence more than the presents. We should not be satisfied only with the attributes of God, when He is offering us His very self. More than we need things, we need God.

'I need Thy Presence every passing hour.' We may need love, peace and healing, but they must never be substitutes for God. Sometimes when these gifts disappear from our lives, when clouds come down and we lose control, it may show what we have set our sights on. It is amazing how many people refuse to believe—or to have a relationship with God—because they did not get what they wanted. They wanted presents, not the Presence. Let us rejoice with the Celtic Church and affirm that we want Him above all else.

> Be Thou my Vision, O Lord of my heart.
> Naught be all else to me, save that Thou art.
> Thou my best thought in the day and the night,
> Waking or sleeping, Thy Presence my light.
>
> Be Thou my wisdom, be Thou my true Word.
> I ever with Thee, and Thou with me, Lord.
> Thou my great Father, and I Thy true son;
> Thou in me dwelling, and I with Thee one.[6]

Patrick, setting out to do battle with the forces that were raised against him at Tara, drew his strength from God, his Companion. Patrick had no doubt about his own weakness and mortality, but neither did he doubt the strength and ability of the Eternal. This would be an encounter that he would make not in his own strength, thank God!

Once again, in this stanza of the 'The Deer's Cry', Patrick is using the Celtic *Caim* to express the encompassing and surrounding of God. Between himself and the crisis he was facing, he saw the Presence and purpose of God. Between the idea and the reality, there was no shadow of doubt, but the Divine Glory. No doubt from this Patrick was given courage and strength, but it was the courage and strength that comes from having a Companion. He was not alone, and at every turn the Almighty was there. Throughout, almost in every line, Patrick turns to God. It is God who pilots, upholds, guides and protects, and it is God's way that lies ahead. The victory does not depend on us alone, but on God.

It is true that God will not do for us what we can do for ourselves, but when we are powerless of ourselves to help ourselves, the Almighty is there. At all times, 'underneath are the everlasting arms'. The writer to the Hebrews suggests that it is an awful thing to fall into the hands of God—but it would be far worse if we could fall out of them.

St Paul saw that it is not in our own merit that we are chosen:

> God chose the foolish things of the world to shame the wise; God chose the weak things of the world to shame the strong.[7]

It is because we are foolish that God can reveal His wisdom through us; because we are weak, His strength can be shown. We have been trained to be self-reliant, self-sufficient. We need to discover again that our sufficiency is of God. We need to learn again to trust Him who watches over us. For the Celt, the God who sees, sees also into the future and deeply into every situation. God keeps an eye on all things.

> The Father who created me
> With eye benign beholdeth me;
> The Son who dearly purchased me
> With eye divine enfoldeth me;
> The Spirit who so altered me
> With eye refining holdeth me;
> In friendliness and love the Three
> Behold me when I bend the knee.[8]

We could go on looking at the Presence, described as ear, hand, way or shield of God. The description does not matter. What matters is the reality of the Presence. What comes across is that Patrick is a friend of God. His God goes with him.

It would be very easy to mock some of the Celtic descriptions of God, to laugh at the crudeness of their words. But no one can belittle their awareness of God in their daily lives. There was for them a Divine immanence that helped them to transcend much that was dull routine and hard labour. They talked naturally to Him as a man or woman talks to a friend. They rejoiced in a closeness and were sure of His help. Through Him, a glory was theirs, a glory that made the world quite a different place, for they were never alone. Whether they needed guidance, a helping hand or a companion, they could turn to the Friend and say, 'God'.

It was this Presence that gave them the ability to undertake adventure and risk. It is the same Presence that gives meaning to mission, for it is only when we can go out, not in our own strength and ideas, but in the power and love of Him who abides, that we have a mission at all.

One of the sad things for our world is that we have allowed God to become remote. We have edged Him out, fixed Him in certain places, and so a glory has departed from the earth. We need to turn around from this far country and then, like the prodigal son, we shall discover that the Father comes to meet us. To discover the Presence is a home-coming, and it is the only way we will be at home in the present.

EXERCISES

1. *Affirm the Presence*—with your lips
   in your mind
   with your heart
   in reality.

2. Use as a daily creed:

   I believe, O God of all gods, that you are
   The Eternal Father of Life.

   I believe, O God of all gods, that you are
   The Eternal Father of Love.

   I believe, O God of all gods, that you are
   The Eternal Father of Peace.

Put the emphasis on the Presence in the present. When you add another attribute instead of Life, Love or Peace, take your time, making yourself aware of that Reality. Know that the gift is there because the Giver is with you.

3. Express again the reality that God is there.

   Between each thought and each action
   place the Presence.
   Between each encounter and event
   place the Presence.

4. Because you are in the Presence, you can rejoice in His 'attributes'. Say and mean each word:

   May the strength of God pilot us,
   May the power of God preserve us,
   May the wisdom of God instruct us,
   May the hand of God protect us,
   May the way of God direct us,
   May the shield of God defend us.[9]

I bind unto myself today
The power of God to hold and lead,
His eye to watch, His might to stay,
His ear to hearken to my need.
The wisdom of my God to teach,
His hand to guide, His shield to ward,
The word of God to give me speech,
His heavenly host to be my guard.

'CLIFFS OF FALL'

'Cliffs of Fall'

I summon today, all these powers between me and those
*   evils,*
Against every cruel merciless power that may oppose my
*   body and soul,*
Against incantations of false prophets,
Against black laws of pagandom,
Against false laws of heretics,
Against craft of idolatry,
Against spells of women and smiths and wizards,
Against every knowledge that corrupts man's body and soul.

Christ to shield me today
Against poisoning, against burning,
Against drowning, against wounding,
So there come to me abundance of reward.

There are days when it is not easy to arise, heavy days
when the world seems to be against us. There are days
when injustice appears to triumph and wickedness flour-
ishes, and it is no use pretending otherwise. Patrick knew
he was engaged in a battle and he would need to call on
all the powers of God if he was to survive.

No matter how fit we are, or how disciplined, there are
days when we are not in control and nothing goes to plan.
Perhaps we may discover later that we never were in control, except over a very small, limited area. To assume we
are in control is one of the illusions in life, and every now
and again that illusion is shattered. There are days when
I know that this life is a very frail and small craft on a
great and stormy sea. I know that I am mortal and could
easily be numbered among the perishing. Then I often

pray the prayer of the Breton fishermen: 'Lord, the sea is so large and my boat is so small.'

Amid the storms and chaos that are part of our existence, I remember the Presence. Perhaps, like the disciples on the Sea of Galilee, I have let Him sleep. It may take some great storm to let me see that I need Him. It is only if we have got to a stage where we cannot save ourselves that we need a Saviour. We are often in such a predicament, if only we would recognise it. The more we live life to the full, the more we launch out and adventure, the more we leave the safety and security of the known, the more we will need a Saviour. If we have never needed a Saviour, we cannot have ventured very far. As the Celt set out, he prayed to Him who is in ultimate command:

> God of the elements, glory to thee
> For the lantern-guide of the ocean wide;
> On my rudder's helm may thine own hand be,
> And thy love abaft on the heaving sea.[1]

For the Celtic Church, the world was a very perilous place. Leaving home and clan for the unknown brought with it many dangers. Usually at dusk the first task would be to light a camp fire—sometimes it may have been a special Paschal fire. It would help to keep wild beasts and the powers of darkness away, although it would announce the travellers' presence to the enemy. Of the coming of Patrick to Tara, we are told: 'They left their vessel in the estuary and went along the land till they came to *Ferta Fer Fiacc* (the graves of Fiacc's men) and Patrick's tent was pitched in that place, and he struck the Paschal fire.'[2] So Patrick announced his presence and roused the opposition.

Very often at night, when the camp fire had burned low, they must have been aware of the eyes that were watching in the dark. The lower the fire burned, the closer came the encircling eyes, waiting for an unguarded moment to pounce on their prey. Very often the darkness must have seemed endless and their little light so small.

When the first missionary came to Lindisfarne from Iona, he returned home because the people were too barbaric. It then became Aidan's turn to bring the light to Northumbria. When Cedd chose the beautiful moors where I live as a site for a monastery, Bede wrote:

> Cedd chose a site for the monastery among some high and remote hills, which seemed more suitable for the dens of robbers and haunts of wild beasts, than for human habitation. His purpose in this was to fulfil the prophecy of Isaiah: 'In the habitation of dragons, where each lay, shall be grass, with reeds and rushes', so that the fruits of good works might spring up where formerly lived only wild beasts, or men who lived like the beasts.[3]

About the time Columba was at Iona, Columbanus was at work on the Continent. After a long training in Ireland, Columbanus wanted to go 'into strange lands'. With twelve companions, he crossed to England and then to Gaul, preaching, teaching and labouring as they went. At first they met with success, but opposition from the heathen and jealous Roman clerics drove them into Switzerland and then Italy.

For the early missionaries, life was heroic and full of adventure. Cormac, the son of Culennan, made his choice:

Shall I choose, O King of mysteries,
After the delight of downy pillows and music,
To go upon the rampart of the sea,
Turning my back on my native land?

Shall I be in poverty in the battle
Through the grace of the King, a King without decay,

Without great honour, without my chariot,
Without gold, or silver, or horse?

Shall I launch my dusky little coracle
On the broad-bosomed glorious ocean?
Shall I go, O King of bright Heaven
Of my own upon the brine?

Whether it be roomy or narrow,
Whether it be severed by crowds or hosts—
O God, wilt thou stand by me
When it comes upon the angry sea?[4]

This was to be the great adventure for many, but more than we know must have met the 'red martyrdom': '. . . others, refusing to accept freedom, died under torture in order to be raised to a better life.'[5] For most, there was little glory or reward for their labours in this world. It was a perpetual struggle to keep the light burning and prevent the Dark Ages from extinguishing them. If the light once went out, so many destructive powers would be let loose.

This is still true today. Now that we live in what is called a post-Christian era, there are dangers that these destructive forces will return. Much of what is in man and society is still very near to the wild beast. The increase of violence in our society and around the world are signs that the darkness is far from conquered. Crime figures soar, assaults and muggings increase. There is no doubt that there are still many 'demons' let loose. If good men do nothing, evil will triumph. If we allow the Light that we have seen to go out of the world, we shall perish.

The opposition that Patrick encountered was very real. At Tara, he was faced with cruel and merciless powers that sought his life. False prophets and all the black arts of pagandom pitted themselves against him, knowing that it was a battle to death. One or the other must go; both could not survive. There was danger from within the Church—from false teachers, heretics and apostates. There were those who opposed the Living God and wanted to continue serving idols; men and women caught in the darkness and seeking to put out the Light. Then there were all sorts of charming things that would distract a man from his work. We may not believe in spells, but there are still many things which captivate us and prevent us from being the people we ought to be, and from doing what we ought to do.

We may feel that mankind is wiser now, and less superstitious; yet whatever name we give to things, there is still much opposition to what is good. In our cleverness, we have found more subtle ways of destruction, more subtle ways of poisoning minds. The powers of evil have in no way diminished in our world. We are still called to be part of the Church Militant here on earth.

Patrick sought protection against every knowledge that corrupts man's body and soul. To us, this may say something about the drug scene and glue-sniffers. It will challenge us about things we eat and drink and perhaps what we inhale—this includes lead in petrol and acid rain. It will ask what we are doing with radioactive waste, about pollution of air and water. It will challenge some types of farming and it will fight against unemployment and world hunger. There will be a need to check television violence and the trade in 'video nasties', and to look carefully at certain forms of advertising and the attitudes that are put forward. There is a constant stream of knowledge coming to us that can corrupt body and soul.

It is no use pretending that all knowledge is good and that we are mature enough to cope with it, for this is not true. We have also discovered ways of manipulation, even of the subconscious. There is subliminal advertising;

there are many 'hidden persuaders'. We hardly know what avenues we are being forced into.

The Age of Reason is quickly fading from the horizon. Very few people see the world as an orderly and controllable place to live in. All around us there are forces that are strange and wild. If our senses and emotions are open, we will discover powers of destruction and disintegration at work in the world and in ourselves. We can deny them, but they do not go away. We have learned that if we force them down into our subconscious, they remain there to haunt us in new and strange ways. Perhaps horror films and violent movies appeal because they are more true to what is in the human psyche than much of the sweetness that is wrongly put forward as a 'way of salvation'. If the Church, or an individual, ignores the forces of disintegration around and within, they will be defeated by them. There are more dangerous things than cigarettes in our lives and homes which should carry a health warning. There are many things that radiate lethal charges which should be approached with the greatest of caution and handled with extreme care. We have learned that, once we have been contaminated by certain things, there is no easy way to be saved.

In the midst of all this, it is very tempting to try to escape, to pretend it does not exist. Sometimes the pursuit of science itself is used as a safety device, a defence against facing the fullness of life. By dealing with controlled experiments in laboratory conditions, we can avoid much of the anxiety that is around outside. Many a scientist lives a life as cloistered as that of a monk. If we choose to deal only with what can be experienced by the five senses and understood by our minds, controlled by our actions, then we must be dealing only with inanimate things—or those that are near to being inanimate. To deal with the predictable is to deal with the fixed. But the deeper the level of being, the less fixed it is, and the more fluid it becomes. We no longer comfortably believe that we live in a tidy universe where things are progressing gently towards the good. Change is occurring at such a rate that all of us are in danger of being swamped by it. Much of the time it seems as if the chaos from which the world was created has made a comeback. The clinically clean and protected men of the laboratory have split the atom. None of us have been spiritually prepared for what they have let loose on mankind. Divisions, disintegration and destruction are very much part of life here on earth.

More and more people are seeking to escape, to avoid the issues, to tranquillise themselves with hyperactivity, science, religion or drugs. That is to retreat from the fullness of life—and it is a very sensible thing to do if there is no God!

We have a Creator who brings order out of chaos, a Saviour who offers life beyond the many deaths and hells of this world, a Spirit who breathes life into the inanimate; we should therefore be able to walk with a little more confidence. We should be the adventurers and explorers. We can live where people take the fullness of life seriously, and yet see that it is not a tragedy. We are able to face the full range and depth of human experience because we are not alone.

> *I arise today*
> *Through God's strength to pilot me: . . .*
> *From snares of devils,*
> *From temptations of vices,*
> *From every one who shall wish me ill,*
> *. . . Christ to shield me today.*

Although the dangers from without were great, Patrick was also aware of dangers that dwell within—those destructive elements we all carry around inside of us:

'Now on that same night, when I was sleeping, Satan assailed me mightily, in such sort as I shall remember as long as I am in the body.'[6] The language may be quaint to us, but he was trying to put into words an experience that was real to him. We may like to change the words and talk of 'nightmare', 'libido', 'subconscious' or whatever, but the experience was something which happened to him.

To ignore our deepest feelings and deny that we have strange desires is to court disaster. Freud has suggested that the price of our so called civilisation has been a great deal of repression, and he questioned whether it was worth it.

It is often when we have been stretched to the limit of our capacities that we find it harder to control that which rises from the subconscious. Gerard Manley Hopkins expresses this well:

No worst, there is none. Pitched past pitch of grief,
More pangs will, schooled at forepangs, wilder
    wring . . .

O the mind, mind has mountains; cliffs of fall
Frightful, sheer, no-man-fathomed. Hold them cheap
May who ne'er hung there. Nor does long our small
Durance deal with that steep deep.[7]

If we do not want to risk, then we have to pretend that the mountains of the mind do not exist. All who want to stretch themselves must face the 'cliffs of fall, frightful, sheer, no-man-fathomed.' For the Christian, the good news is we are not alone. The Christ who descended into the hells of this world is with us and He knows the hearts of men. If we are to scale the mountains of the mind, we are able to do it because He has gone before. He is the Light that is present in the innermost darkness. In many ways we cannot know Him as the Christ until we have got away from our comforts and securities. Unless we have experienced the fact that we are perishable, we do not need a Saviour. Only when we know that we are mortal can we begin to have immortal longings.

We should ask ourselves, 'Are we among the perishing, or do we have a Someone who makes the difference?' The greatest gift that God can give to us is Himself, and nothing can separate us from Him. The fishermen from South Uist knew the perils of the sea but had a strong trust in the Presence. Their 'Ship Consecration' by helmsman and crew could be applied to many situations in life; there is no reason why it should not be used in office or factory instead of ship:

Helmsman:	Be the ship blest.
Crew:	By God the Father blest.
Helmsman:	Be the ship blest.
Crew:	And by God the Son blest.
Helmsman:	Be the ship blest.
Crew:	By God the Spirit blest.
Helmsman:	What can afear With God the Father near?
Crew:	Naught can afear.
Helmsman:	What can afear And God the Son is near?
Crew:	Naught can afear.
Helmsman:	What can afear And God the Spirit near?
Crew:	Naught can afear.
Helmsman:	What care is bred, Being of all o'erhead?
Crew:	No care is bred.
Helmsman:	What care is bred, The King of all o'erhead?

Crew:	No care is bred.
Helmsman:	What care is bred,
	Spirit of all o'erhead?
Crew:	No care is bred.
All:	Being of all,
	The King of all,
	Spirit of all,
	Over our head.
	Eternal fall,
	Near to us sure
	For evermore.[8]

To the gift of the Presence is added the belief that we
'shall not perish but have everlasting life'—'So there come
to me abundance of reward.' We are the sons and daughters of God and 'this mortal will put on immortality'. The
power to face life to the full, to survive its many dangers,
is through the grace of God.

> *I bind unto myself today*
> *The power of God . . .*
> *Against the demon snares of sin,*
> *The vice that gives temptation force,*
> *The natural lusts that war within . . .*
> *Against their fierce hostility*
> *I bind to me these holy powers.*

EXERCISES

1. Know that it is a dark world. See yourself in the darkness. For a moment, let it close around you.

Then see the light coming towards you—the light of Christ, the Lantern of the Father. Know that the darkness cannot put it out. Let the Light fill your life.

Know that you are not alone in the dark, He is with you.

In each dark and troubled situation in your life, let the Light enter.
Say often: 'Yea, though I walk through the valley of the shadow of death, I will fear no evil; for thou art with me.'

Pray: 'Lighten our darkness, we beseech thee, O Lord, and defend us from every peril and danger.'

2. Learn to radiate light.

You can begin in a dark room. Light a candle (or put on a light). Remember: 'It is better to light a small candle than to complain about the darkness.'

As the small light shines in the dark, know that Christ shines in the darkness of your life. Let that Light increase . . . it is the Light of Christ.

Let that Light fill the room where you are sitting, dispelling the fear of the unknown and the darkness.

Let it fill the place where you are—at home, your place of work, the train on which you are travelling.

Know that that Light is spreading out.

The same Light is with your loved ones, your neighbours, your community, the whole country, the world. Pick specific subjects and let the Light be seen in the darkness.

Know that He is there and that His Light should shine.
Learn to be radiant with His Light.

3. Think over these words of Bede:

> Christ is the day-star,
> Who, when the night of this world is past,
> promises and reveals to His saints
> the eternal light of life.

IN HIM WE LIVE

In Him we Live

Christ with me, Christ before me, Christ behind me,
Christ in me, Christ beneath me, Christ above me,
Christ on my right, Christ on my left,
Christ when I lie down, Christ when I sit down, Christ
*   when I arise,*
Christ in the heart of every man who thinks of me,
Christ in the mouth of every one who speaks of me,
Christ in the eye of every one that sees me,
Christ in every ear that hears me.

It has been said that Christianity has not been tried and found wanting, it has never been tried. There are few who take Christ fully at His words: 'I will be with you always, to the end of the age.'[1] Because of this, words are used without meaning, ideas without experience. Christ is treated like a person in a book and in history, rather than as the Living Lord. Because there is no real encounter, we dispense with Him as we would dispense with any other idea, and we are left impoverished.

Patrick lived in awareness of the Presence, sure that Christ was with him and in him. That is faith. Faith can be seen as an act of appropriation, of taking to oneself the reality which others only talk of. Faith occurs when we have a personal encounter with God. Then Christ is no longer treated as a historical character but as the one who comes now: present in the Presence. He stands at the door and knocks. He is close to each of us and ready to answer our call. For us, this is the exciting discovery: 'in Him we live and move and have our being.' We are not people of a book, not even of the Bible, but of the Word, the living

Christ. A poem by the seventeenth century German mystic known as Angelus Silesius warns us:

> Though Christ a thousand times
> In Bethlehem be born,
> If He's not born in thee,
> Thou art still forlorn.
>
> The cross on Golgotha
> Will never save thy soul,
> The cross in thine own heart
> Alone can make thee whole.

Often, in church, when I turn towards the congregation and say, 'The Lord be with you', I hear a very subdued, even dull reply, 'And also with you.' I proclaim, 'The Lord is here,' and there is hardly a glimmer of excitement. Then I wonder what we are doing and saying. To declare the Presence of our God is one of the most exciting things that we can ever do. Every time we declare the Presence, we should thrill with excitement, our hearts should burst with joyful alleluias. It if has become merely a repetitive and dull statement, we should ask ourselves, 'What has happened to us?' To know the Presence can never be dull; if we are dull it is because we are out of touch. We must stop talking about Him; stop searching for Him in books and distant places, and learn that He has already found us and is within. An old Irish quatrain says:

> Going to Rome? Going to Rome?
> 'Twill bring no profit, only trouble,
> The King thou there would quest
> Not found shall be, if he go not in thy breast.[2]

St Augustine's very moving expression of this discovery speaks for us all at some time:

Too late have I loved Thee, O Beauty, so ancient yet

ever new, too late have I loved Thee! Lo! Thou wast within and I without, and there I mis-shapen was running in search of Thee amidst those lovely shapes which Thou hadst formed. Thou wast with me, and I was not with Thee . . . Thou didst call, shout, shatter my deafness; Thou didst flash, shine, scatter my blindness. And I drew in my breath and I pant for Thee, I tasted Thee and I hunger and thirst. Thou didst touch me and I burned for Thy peace.[3]

The same Christ is still passing by; it is only our blindness that prevents us from seeing Him. He is ready to hear us and to come to us. We must not be put off by the things that crowd in upon us. Day by day we need to call upon His Presence. We need to shout out like Bartimaeus: 'Jesus! Son of David! Take pity on me.'[4] We need to learn the 'Jesus Prayer'; to call often on His name, for the Lord is at hand. Patrick had obviously learned such a prayer when he called upon the Lord several times in a day. Perhaps in this section of his Hymn we get a glimpse not of one prayer, but of many prayers—short affirmations of the Presence at all times. We, too, need to stop talking about Him and to talk to Him.

Christ with me

Christ, this is not a request but a fact.
You, Christ, are here and with me now.
Christ, open my eyes to Your Presence
       open my ears to Your call,
       open my heart to Your love,
       open my will to Your command.

Christ, you have promised You will be with me 'always, to the end of the age'. My imagination may fail, but Your

Presence is real. My eyes may be dim, but You are still there.

Christ, I call upon your Name, for You are with me. I am never alone, never without help, never without a friend, for I dwell in You and You in me! 'Yea, though I walk through the valley of the shadow of death, I will fear no evil; for You are with me.'

Christ before me

Christ, You have gone before me to prepare a place for me, that where You are, I may be also. There is nowhere I can journey that You have not travelled:

> If I went up to heaven, you would be there;
> if I lay down in the world of the dead, you would be
> there.
> If I flew away beyond the east,
> or lived in the farthest place in the west,
> you would be there to lead me,
> you would be there to help me.[5]

Christ, I do not know what lies ahead, but I do know *Who* is with me.

Christ, I do not know where I shall end up, but I know *Who* is there before me.

Christ, the future is not fully unknown for You are there before me.

Christ behind me

Christ, You are behind me to protect me from evil, defending me from all that would creep up on me. You stand between me and all that seeks to defile me.

Christ, You enter through the door of the past with Your love and forgiveness. You can come where doors are closed and bring light and peace.

Christ, I put my hand in Yours, for I am afraid; I bring memories that hurt and a past that pains, for Your healing and renewal.

Christ, come enter through the door of the past;
>   into the remembered and the forgotten,
>   into the joys and sorrows,
>   into the recording room of memories,
>   into the secret room of sin,
>   into the hidden room of shame,
>   into the mourning room of sorrow,
>   into the bright room of love,
>   into the joyful room of achievement.

Come Christ, enter
>   into the fibre of our being,
>   into the conscious and subconscious,
>   into the roots of personality.

'Cleanse me from my secret faults and renew a right spirit within me.'

Christ in me

Christ, there is no need for long pilgrimages, for You are within. Christ, help me to make the journey inwards and discover Your Presence in me. In this alone is there any dignity that will last. You, O Christ, have chosen to be born in me.

>   Christ born in a stable
>   is born in me.
>   Christ accepted by shepherds
>   accepts me.

> Christ receiving the wise men
> receives me.
> Christ revealed to the nations
> be revealed in me.
> Christ dwelling in Nazareth
> You dwell in me.

Christ, grant that people may look at me and see Your Presence.

Christ, help me to know that I am called to be the body of Christ.

> Christ has no hands but our hands
> To do His work today.
> Christ has no feet but our feet
> To speed men on their way.
> Christ has no lips but our lips
> To tell men why He died.
> Christ has no love but our love
> To win men to His side.

Christ, may Your work be fulfilled in us, and Your Presence revealed in us.

Christ beneath me

Christ, no matter how far I have fallen, You are there also; 'Underneath are the everlasting arms.'

Christ, I look at the hands that uphold me and I see the print of nails. The hands that bear me up know pain and sorrow. You, Lord, know the betrayals and rejections of this world.

Christ, 'if I descend into hell You are there also'. You experienced the many hells of this world. You have descended so that You can lift us up. In all dangers, You are there to support us:

In the storms of life,
In the sinking of the disciple,
In the scorning and rejecting,
In the betrayals and denials,
In the hells and crucifixions,
In the ebbing out of life,
Christ beneath me.
And I know that You are the Risen Lord of Life.

Christ above me

Christ, risen and ascended Lord.
Christ, above all things, You came down to lift us up.
Christ, I know that You walk with me in the storms, and yet in a strange way You are above the waves.
Christ, I will not sink if You will lift me up.
Christ, as You have ascended, help me also in heart and mind to ascend and with You dwell forever.

When waves roar and winds increase,
Lift me, Christ, to Your peace.
When the way is dark and the night cold,
Keep me, Christ, in Your hold.
My faith is weak, my vision dim,
Save me, Christ, I cannot swim.
Let Your hand reach down to me,
Lift me from this perplexity.
Ascended Christ, with mighty hand,
Bring me safe again to land.

Christ on my right

Christ with all who are dexterous, all creators and beautifiers of our world.

Christ with all artists and craftsmen, all who enrich our lives working for the good of creation.

Christ in all that comes to life this day, all that grows, blossoms, increases.

Christ in all that is peaceful, joyful and hopeful.

Christ revealed in glory.

Christ in whoever approaches me from the right.

Christ in my neighbour, Christ in hearts of all that love me.

Christ, whoever is at my right. You are in them.

Christ on my left

Christ, there with the sinister, seeking to save.

Christ there with all that would seek to diminish, destroy this day. With all who are burdened and heavy laden.

Christ with all whose lives are drained and emptied this day, with the suffering and poor, the oppressed and the tyrannised.

Christ with all who will die this day.

Christ in whoever approaches me from the left.

Christ in the stranger. Christ in those who rise against me.

Christ to be discovered in all who oppose or hate me.

Christ in all who hinder and exhaust me.

Christ, whoever is at my left. You are in them.

Christ when I lie down

Christ, I come to You when I am weary and heavy laden knowing that You will refresh me. When life lays me low, You will lift me up. 'I will lay me down in peace . . . for it is Thou, Lord, only that makest me dwell in safety.'[6]

> I am going now into the sleep,
> Be it that I in health shall wake;
> If death be to me in deathly sleep,
> Be it that in thine own arm's keep.
> O God of grace, to new life I wake,
> O be it in thy dear arm's keep,
> O God of grace, that I shall awake.
>
> Be my soul on thy right hand, O God,
> O Thou King of the heaven of heaven;
> Thou it was who didst buy with Thy blood,
> Thine the life for my sake was given;
> Encompass thou me this night, O God,
> That no harm, no mischief be given.[7]

Christ, watch me while I sleep. Let me learn to trust in You.

> Watch thou, dear Lord, with those who wake, or watch, or weep tonight, and give thine angels charge over those who sleep. Tend thy sick ones, O Lord Christ. Rest thy weary ones. Bless thy dying ones. Soothe thy suffering ones. Pity thine afflicted ones. And for all thy love's sake.[8]

Christ when I sit down

Christ when I cease activity,
Christ when I quieten the mind,
Christ when I still the tongue,

Christ when I calm the heart,
Christ in quiet,
Christ, teach me to be still and know that You are God.

Christ when I sit down at table,
Christ the uninvited guest,
Christ when I sit down alone, my companion and friend,
Christ when I sit down in company—where two or three
   are gathered, You are there.
When I sit down in conference,
Christ in mouth of friend and stranger.

Christ when I arise

Christ when I arise to the new day,
Christ when I arise to the new opportunity,
Christ when I arise above temptation,
Christ when I arise above the storms,
Christ when I arise from all that would depress me,
Christ when I arise from death,
Christ when I arise to Your Presence.

> Thanks be to Thee ever, O Gentle Christ,
> That Thou has raised me freely from the black,
> And from the darkness of last night
> To the kindly light of this day.[9]

Christ in the heart of every man who thinks of me

Christ, You are to be found in my loved ones.

Christ, help me to set out on the voyage of discovery that
he who loves is born of God and knows God. The discovery that as I do it to the least of these, I do it to You.

Christ, let me see Your call in the call for love, in the plea
of the poor and needy.

Christ, when we truly love, we open our lives not only to another but to that Great Other which is You.

Christ in the heart of every man, even those who as yet do not know or love You, help me to seek You and others to find You.

Christ in mouth of every one who speaks of me

'Christ in mouth of friend and stranger.'
Christ, make me attentive to the word, that I may hear the Word.
Christ, make me listen to the other, that I may hear the Other.
Christ, when words fail and communication breaks down, You are still there to keep us together.
Christ, when two or three are gathered together in conversation, You are there.
Christ, speak to me in the voice of a friend, in the chatter of a child, in the words of a stranger.

Christ in the eye of every one that sees me

Christ, let me see You in others.
Christ, let others see You in me.
Christ, let me see:

You are the caller
You are the poor
You are the stranger at my door.

You are the wanderer
The unfed
You are the homeless
With no bed.

You are the man
Driven insane

You are the child
Crying in pain.

You are the other who comes to me
Open my eyes that I may see.[10]

Christ, grant that in me others may see

Your glory,
Your grace,
Your goodness,
Your Presence,
For without You, I am nothing.

Christ in every ear that hears me

Christ, You are there before I speak,
Help me to respect You.
Christ, You are present in the listener,
Let me reveal You, or be revealed to me.
Christ, may my words not hide
You the Word.

Christ is here,
Christ is there,
Christ is everywhere.
Christ above,
Christ below,
Christ along the path I go. Alleluia. Amen.

EXERCISES

1. Pray regularly the 'Jesus Prayer':
   'Lord Jesus Christ, Son of God, have mercy on me.'

Learn to call upon Him often, for He is there. Quietly say, 'Christ with me'. Repeat this many times in the day. Know that you are not making Him come, He is already there. You are seeking to be more aware of Him.

2. Learn to see Christ in others. Remind yourself that he is to be found in friend and stranger. You are on a voyage of discovery. Before each meeting with people, each encounter, whilst travelling on the bus or tube or train, pray that He may reveal Himself to you.

3. Learn to be Christ to others
A small girl found Thorwalden's 'Christ' in a deserted house. She brought it to her father and said, 'It has no hands.' The father raised the girl to his knee and told her with a quiet assurance, 'Then you will have to be his hands.'
You are called to be a sharer in His salvation. Seek ways to be the hands, the feet, the lips, the mind of Christ. Pray that He may work now through you.

4. Use each little phrase of this verse as an 'arrow prayer' and affirmation. This is a reality we are so often blind to; pray that you may see.

> *Christ be with me, Christ within me,*
> *Christ behind me, Christ before me,*
> *Christ beside me, Christ to win me,*
> *Christ to comfort and restore me,*
> *Christ beneath me, Christ above me,*
> *Christ in quiet, Christ in danger,*
> *Christ in hearts of all that love me,*
> *Christ in mouth of friend and stranger.*

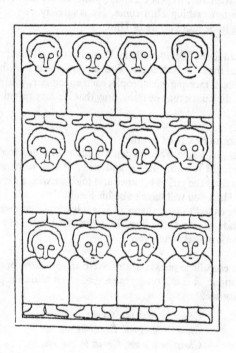

THE CRY
OF THE DEER

P. Daigle.

The Cry of the Deer

I arise today
Through a mighty strength, the invocation of the Trinity,
Through belief in the threeness,
Through confession of the oneness
Of the Creator of Creation.

There is a feeling that we have been here before. It is as if we had traced around a Celtic interlacing pattern with all its ups and downs and come back to where we had started. But it is not the end; there is no end. There is no end because we are involved in and immersed in the Eternal. For all our travels, all our readings, we do not escape the Presence—nor our yearning to be more aware of God. It is because of our seeking to discover Him in the pattern of life, that we have discovered He has made it endless. We have discovered that: 'We come from God, we belong to God. We return to God.' If we seem to be back to where we began, at least let it be with a new awareness:

> We shall not cease from exploration,
> And the end of all our exploring
> Will be to arrive where we started
> And to know the place for the first time.[1]

We arise today. Today we discover God through His creation; in the mysteries of the universe, the great mystery of God calls out to us, drawing us towards Him in wonder and awe. We meet Christ incarnate. Whenever we encounter another, the Great Other seeks to meet us. We dwell in the Spirit and He is revealed in His inspiration. We dwell in Him, and so He enthuses us. This has been so throughout the history of mankind and it is ours to experience today. Even this is just a beginning; we will arise again and again, not only today and tomorrow, but again into Eternity through the mighty strength of God. We have walked into the 'never-ending story', for we have discovered that we are part of the Eternal. Life can never be the same again. What God has done, He will continue to do in us and through us. We can express our trust in the Eternal in affirming this unchanging attitude towards us:

As He is
He was:
As He was
He is.
He shall be
As he is
And was,
The Eternal
Forever
So be it
Amen.
The Forever
Eternal
So be it
Amen.[2]

Yet there will still be times in this life when the pattern 'goes under'. At such times of distress and loneliness we may lose our vision, or feel that we are in a far country greatly removed from the Father. At such times the heart longs for love, and our spirit goes in search of a presence. Then we begin to wander; we are dis-eased and restless. It is hard then to believe. Yet whether we believe or not, He is still there. We should make quiet efforts to remind ourselves of the Presence, to know that for all our wander-

ings we need not seek Him because we have already
'arrived'.

When on holiday, I am often tempted to travel too much
and seek to see as much as I can. I want to see around the
next corner, to climb another hill to see another vista, to
seek out yet another peaceful scene. I may on such
occasions cover a great amount of ground, but there is a
danger of never knowing when I have arrived: of something in me searching out beauty, glory and peace, travelling on, when Beauty, Glory and Peace are being offered
to me here and now, today. I cry out like the deer that
seeks water:

> As a deer longs for a stream of cool water,
> So I long for you, O God.
> I thirst for you, the living God . . .
> Why am I so sad?
> Why am I so troubled?
> I will put my hope in God,
> and once again I will praise him,
> My saviour and my God.[3]

My inner restlessness is like the cry of the deer in its thirst,
and without that longing being met, I will perish. Just as
nothing else can satisfy the deer, nothing else can quench
our thirst. Our hearts were made for the Eternal and
nothing but the Eternal will ever fill them to the full. St
Augustine has rightly said: 'Lord, our hearts are restless
until they rest in Thee.'

Sadly, our times too often try to fill the heart with trivial
pursuits and to dull the cry of the deer. As long ago as
1802 Wordsworth wrote:

> The human mind is capable of being excited without
> the application of gross and violent stimulants; and he
> must have a very faint perception of beauty and dignity

143

who does not know this . . . For a multitude of causes, unknown to former times, are now acting with a combined force to blunt the discriminating powers of the mind, and unfitting it for all voluntary exertion, to reduce it to a state of almost savage torpor. The most effective of these causes are the great national events which are daily taking place, and the increasing accumulation of men in cities, where the uniformity of their occupations produces a craving for extraordinary incident which the rapid communication of intelligence hourly gratifies.[4]

Little did Wordsworth know of what was to come: telephone, radio and television were unheard of. But he was not unaware of things that can disturb a man's heart and mind. He saw the dangers of mass communication if man was unprepared to cope with it.

Do we see in the boredom of the young, with its violence and drug-taking, a genuine 'cry of the deer'? A sign of people who have lost the Presence? If life does not have a pattern, a story, it has no meaning; it becomes at best 'a tale told by an idiot'. People are lashing out in many ways against meaningless existence. Life is a grave matter and therefore very serious unless we discover the glorious liberty of the children of God, that today we can arise.

Often it will need a definite turning to a new direction of thinking and looking—what the New Testament calls 'repentance'—a complete turn about. Like many a prodigal son or daughter, we need to make the decision, 'I will arise and go to my Father;' to discover that we have a home to go to, because we belong to God. To discover that it is in our own home, in our own street, in our own work, that He offers us the beauty, glory and peace we have been in search of. The Presence is given with the territory; He is where we are. We are not at the end, but at a new beginning. If there is an end, it is expressed in the words: 'Journeys end in lovers meeting.'

In the discovery that we are loved by the Eternal love, life has meaning; many of our frustrations and angers immediately disappear when we know that we are here for a purpose and that we are important, because He loves us. That serious life is flooded with a comic relief that helps us to arise today. That the things which once set out to pull us down and destroy us can now be laughed at, for in Him we are more than conquerors. In what is a very grave situation, the Christian is able to laugh. So, as the Hebridean crofters went out to work that could be dangerous and was certainly often dull, they would chant:

> With God be my walking this day,
> With Christ be my walking this day,
> With Spirit my walking this day,
> The Threefold all-kindly my way:
> Ho, ho, ho! The Threefold all-kindly I pray.

> My shielding this day be from bane,
> My shielding this night be from pain,
> Ho! Ho! soul and body, the twain,
> By Father, Son, Spirit, amain;
> By Father's, by Son's, and by Holy Ghost's sain.

> The Father be he shielding me,
> And be God the Son shielding me,
> The Spirit be he shielding me,
> As Three and as One let them be:
> Ho, ho, ho! as Three and as One Trinity.[5]

It is once we have learned to be at home with God that we are at home anywhere. The Celtic pilgrims were not restless, but restless until they found the place where He wanted them to be. Once they found His Presence in the place, they sought to dwell there and let Him be revealed there. In our turn, each person has to find his own place. Once found, we then are able to discover Him in all places. There must be a starting place, but there is no end. The Shaker Hymn gives this advice:

'Tis the gift to be simple,
'Tis the gift to be free,
'Tis the gift to come down where we ought to be,
And when we have found the place just right,
'Twill be in the valley of love and delight.

It is then that we discover that He has been there and is there all the time. It was just that we were unaware, did not give our attention to Him:

. . . being attentive to the times of the day: when the birds began to sing, and the deer came out of the morning fog, and the sun came up. The reason why we don't take time is a feeling that we have to keep moving. This is a real sickness. We live in the fullness of time. Every moment is God's own good time, His *kairos*. The whole thing boils down to giving ourselves in prayer a chance to realise that we have what we seek. We don't have to rush after it. It was there all the time, and if we give it time, it will make itself known to us.[6]

We are never done. God is ever seeking to reveal Himself and be made known to us. When a couple are married, their marriage is not completed on their wedding day, it only begins then. Ideally, it is a relationship that they will be working out for the rest of their lives; they will be attentive to each other and not take each other for granted. So it is with our relationship with God. Once begun, it does not end; because it is a relationship, it is never completed, never done.

It is a pity that when parents talk of baptism, they talk of having their child 'done'. We need to discover once again that baptism is not a once-and-for-all event, it is something we must be working at and enjoying continually. We need to see baptism as an immersing in the Presence. When Patrick was faced with the opposing forces at Tara, he reminded himself of his immersion; not of a past baptism, but of the Triune God in whom he was immersed at that very moment. It was this immersion in God and not in his own abilities, that gave Patrick the power to arise. The whole of 'The Deer's Cry' can be seen to be an attempt to become a little more aware of Him 'in whom we live and move and have our being', and to rejoice in His Presence. Baptism is to be total immersion, not in water, but in Him. Not once, but each day:

> The Lord is here
> His Spirit is with us.
>
> We need not fear
> His Spirit is with us.
>
> We are surrounded by love
> His Spirit is with us.
>
> We are immersed in peace
> His Spirit is with us.
>
> We abide in hope
> His Spirit is with us.
>
> We travel in faith
> His Spirit is with us.
>
> We live in Eternity
> His Spirit is with us.
>
> The Lord is here
> His Spirit is with us.

EXERCISES

1. Seek to discover the patterns and purpose of your life. Whether you are up or down, remember He is there. Know that life has no end and that nothing can separate you from the love of God.

If life appears to have no meaning or purpose, know at least that you are created by His love and He loves you.

2. Practise total immersion—see that every event of your life, every thought and deed and word is immersed in Father, Son and Holy Spirit. Use the words of the Baptism service: 'I baptise (immerse) you . . . in the name of the Father and of the Son and of the Holy Spirit.'
Let baptism become a living reality for you:

> *I bind unto myself the name,*
> *The strong name of the Trinity,*
> *By Invocation of the same.*
> *The Three in One, and One in Three,*
> *Of whom all nature hath creation;*
> *Eternal Father, Spirit, Word;*
> *Praise to the Lord of my Salvation*
> *Salvation is of Christ the Lord.*

And 'here, now, always':

> May the Father everlasting
> Himself take you, round you casting
> His own gen'rous arm engrasping.
> His own gen'rous hand enclasping.[7]

NOTES

Introduction

1 This date, later than previously thought, is suggested in Charles Thomas, *Celtic Britain*, Thames and Hudson 1986, p.126
2 Arnold Marsh, tr. *St Patrick's Writings: Confessions*, Dundalk, Dunalgan
3 John Osborne, *Look Back in Anger*, Faber and Faber 1957
4 *Confessions*
5 C.P.S. Clarke, *Everyman's Book of Saints*, Mowbray 1914

The Hymn of St Patrick

1 From Kuno Meyer, *Selections from Ancient Irish Poetry*, 1928
2 Appears in many modern hymnals

Strength through Faith

1 See David Adam, *The Edge of Glory*, Triangle/SPCK 1985, p.8
2 Romans 8.31, 38–9, Good News Bible
3 Matthew 11.28 GNB
4 2 Corinthians 4.7–9 GNB
5 David Gascoyne, 'Fragments towards a *religio poetae*', *Collected Poems*, Oxford University Press 1965
6 See *The Edge of Glory*, p.76

To See Christ

1 John 1.14 Authorised Version
2 Matthew 25.40 GNB
3 Quoted in Victor Gollancz, *A Year of Grace*, Gollancz 1950
4 The *Edge of Glory*, p.34
5 Teilhard de Chardin, *Le Milieu Divin*, Fontana 1964, p.145

Death is Not Fatal

1 Ann Savage, trs., *The Anglo-Saxon Chronicle*, Macmillan 1984
2 *Principles*, Society of Sacred Mission Press, 1930
3 G.R.D. McLean, *Poems of the Western Highlanders*, SPCK 1961, pp.90, 89 and 87
4 Psalm 23.4 AV

'Let Loose in the World'

1 *The Oxford Book of Carols*, Oxford University Press 1928, no. 149
2 Luke 24.5–6 GNB
3 *Poems of the Western Highlanders*, p.275
4 ibid., p.107
5 ibid., p.339
6 ibid., p.234
7 ibid., p.10
8 ibid., p.103
9 ibid., p.415
10 *The Edge of Glory*, p.35

The Christ who Comes

1 Hebrews 11.24–6 GNB
2 Matthew 25.34 GNB
3 Mrs Rundle Charles, *Te Deum Laudamus*, SPCK 1887
4 ibid.
5 *Poems of the Western Highlanders*, p.46
6 ibid., p.425
7 1 John 1.8–9 GNB
8 *Poems of the Western Highlanders*, p.270
9 Brendan Kennelly, ed. *The Penguin Book of Irish Verse*, 'Prayer for Recollection', Penguin 1970, p.52

The Communion of the Saints

1 Peter Berger, *A Rumour of Angels*, Penguin 1970, p.119
2 Hebrews 13.1 GNB
3 Matthew 10.40 GNB
4 See Genesis 18.1–15
5 N.J. White, *St Patrick, His Writings and Life*, Dublin 1920
6 *Confessions*, para 10
7 *Carmina Gadelica* Vol.III, 153
8 *The Penguin Book of Irish Verse*, 'Prayer for Recollection', p.51
9 Philippians 4.4–8 GNB
10 *The Book of Common Prayer* 1662, from the Communion service

The Earth is the Lord's

1   Matthew Arnold, 'The Grande Chartreuse'
2   Quoted in Lucy Menzies, *Saint Columba of Iona*, J.M. Dent 1920
3   See *The Edge of Glory*, p.90
4   Elizabeth Barrett Browning, 'Aurora Leigh'
5   *Le Milieu Divin*, pp.64,66
6   ibid., p.112
7   *Poems of the Western Highlanders*, p.7
8   ibid., p.222
9   ibid., p.255
10 William Blake, 'Auguries of Innocence'

The Presence of God

1   Clifton Wolters trs., *The Cloud of Unknowing*, Penguin Classics 1961 chapter 4
2   ibid., chapter 6
3   *The Edge of Glory*, p.7
4   *Poems of the Western Highlanders*. p.103
5   See *The Edge of Glory*, p.64
6   8th-century Irish hymn, trs. Mary Byrne and Eleanor Hull. Appears in many modern hymnals
7   1 Corinthians 1.27 New International Version
8   *Poems of the Western Highlanders*, p.133
9   See *The Edge of Glory*, p.85

'Cliffs of Fall'

1 *Poems of the Western Highlanders*, p.371
2 Whitley Stokes ed., *The Tripartite Life of St Patrick*, 1877. Vol. 1, p.41
3 Bede, *Ecclesiastical History*, Leo Sherley-Price trs, Penguin 1955, Book III, 23
4 Kuno Meyer, quoted in Leslie Hardinge, *The Celtic Church in Britain*, SPCK 1972, pp. 14–15
5 Hebrews 11.35 GNB
6 *Confessions*
7 Gerard Manley Hopkins, 'No Worst, there is None'
8 *Poems of the Western Highlanders*, p.367

In Him we Live

1 Matthew 28.20 GNB
2 Kuno Meyer, *Selections from Ancient Irish Poetry*, 1928
3 St Augustine, *Confessions*, X.27
4 Mark 10.46–7 GNB
5 Psalm 139.7–10 GNB
6 Psalm 4.9 *Book of Common Prayer*
7 *Poems of the Western Highlanders*, p.415
8 St Augustine
9 Alexander Carmichael, ed. *Carmina Gadelica*, Vol. III, p.29
10 See *The Edge of Glory*, p.34

1 T.S. Eliot, *Four Quartets*, 'Little Gidding', Faber and Faber 1942
2 *The Edge of Glory*, p.10
3 Psalm 42.1–2,5 GNB
4 William Wordsworth, Preface to *Lyrical Ballads*, 1802
5 *Poems of the Western Highlanders*, p.57
6 Thomas Merton, A Hidden Wholeness, p.49
7 *Poems of the Western Highlanders*, p.103

Also published by
TRiΛNGlE

THE EDGE OF GLORY:
Prayers in the Celtic tradition
by David Adam

A simplicity, a directness, a freshness, a spirituality is the essence of this book of prayers which can be for private, group or congregational use. They convey 'the abiding presence that never leaves us or forsakes us'.

Church News

Simple, yet deep, prayers which bring with them an atmosphere of the immanence of God, and do truly touch 'the edge of glory'.

Family Life Newsline

It is a style that beautifully combines God's glory with everyday events. Containing prayers for individual devotions and corporate worship, they all express joyful faith in God.

Christian Family

Apart from the prayers which are very evocative of a mood of peace and acceptance, rooted in the ordinary things of daily life, there are some beautiful line drawings and illustrations in the Celtic style.

Ely Review

TIDES AND SEASONS

Modern prayers in the Celtic tradition

by David Adam

Once again David Adam draws from the rich store of Celtic spirituality insights which speak to our own condition. The prayers he has written for this book echo the rhythms of creation which find their parallels in our spiritual lives. The movement of the tides – incoming, full flood, ebb tide, low tide – are linked to the cycle of the year, the seasons of life, and the highs and lows of our own experience.

'A collection of prayers drawn from the Celtic tradition which have an astonishing capacity to speak to and from our deepest levels of being.' *Parish News*

'The thought of these prayers is immediately attractive, often beautiful, with an incantatory lilt. The book, decorated with drawings in Celtic style, will be gratefully welcomed by all who, with David Adam, have come under the spell of prayer in this tradition.'

Neville Ward in the *Church Times*

'This is a joy-giving book.' *Orthodox News*

Praying with
HIGHLAND CHRISTIANS

G. R. D. McLean

Foreword by Sally Magnusson

A selection of prayers from G. R. D. McLean's translations of traditional Gaelic poems, *Poems of the Western Highlanders*. Though they arise out of a social structure now largely vanished, they deal with the unchanging basics of human life – with bodily needs, the daily round, family love, our fears and temptations and the need for security.

'A refreshing reminder of the great riches of our own heritage . . . Page after page vibrates with a 'glory' which for many has passed away from the earth.'
David Adam

'It is a privilege to pray with these Celtic Christians. Their conversations with the God they loved all those years ago must surely enhance our own, just as their humanity and their faith can only enlarge ours.'
Sally Magnusson

TRI∆NGLE

Books
can be obtained from
all good bookshops.
In case of difficulty,
or for a complete list of our books,
contact:
SPCK Mail Order
36 Steep Hill
Lincoln
LN2 1LU
(tel: 0522 527 486)